Country Roads
~ of ~
NORTH CAROLINA

*A Guide Book
from Country Roads Press*

Country Roads
~ of ~
# NORTH CAROLINA

Glenn Morris

Illustrated by
Clifford Winner

Country Roads Press
CASTINE · MAINE

Country Roads of North Carolina

© 1994 by Glenn Morris. All rights reserved.

Published by Country Roads Press
P.O. Box 286, Lower Main Street
Castine, Maine 04421

Text and cover design by Edith Allard.
Cover art by Victoria Sheridan.
Illustrations by Cliff Winner.
Typesetting by Camden Type 'n Graphics.

ISBN 1-56626-067-1

Library of Congress Cataloging-in-Publication Data
Morris, Glenn.
    Country roads of North Carolina / Glenn Morris ; illustrator, Cliff Winner.
       p. cm.
    Includes index.
    ISBN 1-56626-067-1 : $9.95
    1. North Carolina—Guidebooks. 2. Automobile travel—North Carolina—Guidebooks. I. Title.
F252.3.M65 1994
917.5604'43—dc20   94-14329
                                            CIP

Printed in the United States of America.
10 9 8 7 6 5 4 3 2 1

To Mom and Dad, who taught me that all wrong turns turn out all right.

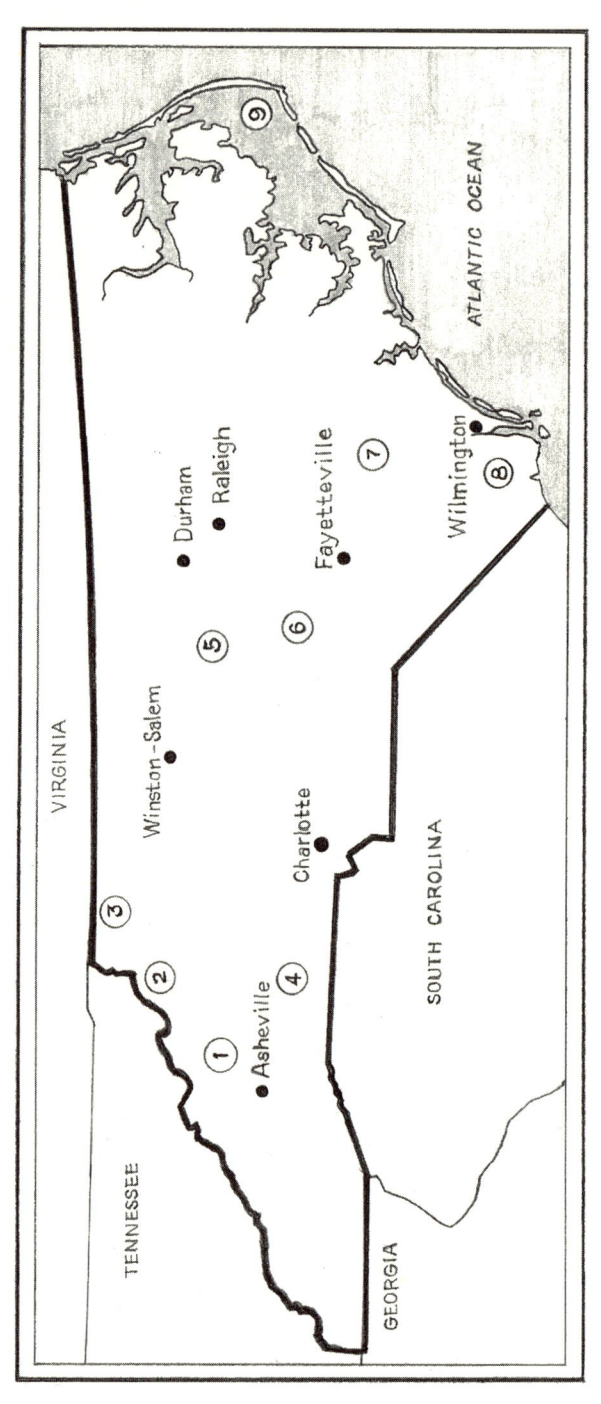

Contents
(& Key to North Carolina Country Roads)

	Introduction	ix
1	The Craggys, The Blacks, and the Highlands of Roan	1
2	The Ski Country Without Snow	20
3	New River Christmas Tree Country	33
4	A Cool Glide at the End of the Ride	50
5	Old Greensboro–Chapel Hill Road and Some Extras	65
6	The Long-Needle Loop: Sight-seeing in the Sandhills	75
7	Lowlands Crossed by Highlanders	92
8	Down by the River and Back Up Again	110
9	Water, Wind, and Sand: Along the Outer Banks	128
	Index	145

Introduction

The following fact is noted in small type on the North Carolina state transportation map: "North Carolina's highway system is the largest state-maintained network."

I will not contest the claim. After these delightful explorations, when I look at the map I see the proverbial roads less traveled—by me. Visitors and residents alike would be better served if the state printed this additional truth-in-witticism on the map: Warning: North Carolina has more country roads than you have time.

Amen.

In its wildest maneuverings, a spider couldn't spin the web that's a North Carolina road map. There are so many glorious little black or red numbered routes to travel between any given places in the state that it boggles the mind. You can't see or do it all, so I do what I can and wonder what I'm missing.

North Carolina is the country's tenth most populous state; thankfully, folks are spread around a bit. The geography and demographics are such that no major city dominates highways or sets a tone for the rest of the state.

There is what I prefer to call the "Great Arc," a belt of cities along I-85 and I-40 curving across the middle of the state from Charlotte to Raleigh. Some years ago, I described this configuration of roads and cities as a place you can dove hunt within beeper range. This still beeps true, although many of the fields that once grew millet now grow subdivisions.

Introduction

The simple fact is that North Carolina is rural. Because of the interstate highway system, what once were the major routes of commerce—such as U.S. highways—today are relegated to a more secondary status. So much the better, for roads such as US 1 on the way to Southern Pines from Raleigh are wonderful drives, more properly country in feeling and passage than their routing designation might lead you to believe. The same is true of US 64 west from Cary.

US 64 is, in fact, the extreme in a state of extremes, wandering the entire 543 miles between the communities referred to as North Carolina's east-west bookends—Manteo and Murphy. Manteo, on the coast, has a briny air about it; Murphy has its head in mountain mists.

North Carolina's physical blessings—the extremely mountainous west and the extremely incised coastline in the east—have historically precluded rapid and easy transit. Most of the roads are literally farm-to-market roads. Today, although the farms may be agribusinesses and the markets national instead of local, the means haven't changed the ways too much at all.

There are some laments: one of them is that when you have lots of places where people can "get away from it all," everybody tries to do just that. In the blink of a decade, stoplights replace stop signs and two lanes become five and everybody can get away to the same place at once.

The nine tours in this book are based on the premise that how you go somewhere is at least as important as where you go. The question "Is it worth the trip?" is flipped to read, "The trip is worth it." The journey becomes the destination, if for no other reason than it's a chance to see something new.

What is the value of a crossroads store with a handpainted soft drink sign, the burnished orange of a sassafras tree in fall, tobacco drying in a barn, or a long-needle pine whispering in a breeze? How much can it mean to chance by a meadow or stream that for a few minutes or hours can belong to you and nobody else in the world? North Carolina's country roads are dense with such gifts waiting for unwrapping. Keep in mind when you go, if you don't have to be somewhere, you can't get lost.

1 ~ The Craggys, The Blacks, and the Highlands of Roan

From Asheville ascend to the Blue Ridge Parkway and head north. Exit the parkway onto State 80 and follow it north to US 19E. Head east to Spruce Pine. Take State 226 north to Bakersville, then follow State 261 to Roan Mountain.

Highlights: *The Folk Art Center; Craggy Gardens; Mount Mitchell; Pisgah National Forest; historic Camp Alice; the Mount Mitchell Golf Course; tubing on the South Toe River; the renowned Penland School of Crafts; and Roan Mountain.*

The southern Appalachians crumple and wrinkle through parts of six states, but they reach a zenith along the North Carolina–Tennessee border. In this airy sweep of countless summits, one massive rounded shoulder, fifty-one miles northeast of Asheville, rises above the others to wear the accolade "garden of the gods." On Roan Mountain in late June, heaven meets earth with a floral handshake that is second to none. More than 600 acres of native rhododendron bloom—no, erupt—in a rose-purple explosion.

There is some country in North Carolina so magnificent that other states surely must have been shortchanged when the natural goodies were allocated. The focus of this tour is Roan Mountain, a must for anyone who loves wild and free places. The bonus is the country you must pass through to reach Spruce Pine, the jumping-off point for Roan Mountain. I suggest you approach Spruce Pine from the south, by way of the Blue Ridge Parkway.

Some of the highlights of the approaches could make tours in their own right. This tour could be combined with elements from the Ski Country Without Snow tour, in the next chapter.

Allow two overnights for this tour, unless you live in Asheville, in which case most of the sights can be explored in two long days and one overnight. Camping is an obvious option.

Bring comfortable shoes. The best things to see require some walking to reach.

The Blue Ridge Parkway north from Asheville to Spruce Pine is packed with wonderful side trips and, on a clear day, grand views.

One of the most pleasant settings along the parkway is just outside of Asheville, one mile north of the parkway junction with US 70, at milepost 382. The Folk Art Center, a ten-year-old, 30,500-square-foot glass and wood building, is an immense showcase for one of the premier organizations of artisans in the country, the Southern Highland Handicraft Guild, with more than 700 members.

With the building as host and the sixty-year-old guild as caterer, you are served some of the finest traditional and contemporary crafts from mountain artisans from several states.

Special exhibits focus on theme shows of members' work; other space in the building is devoted to sales and demonstrations of jewelry and furniture making.

The Craggys, The Blacks, and the Highlands of Roan

Head north from the Folk Art Center, through Craven Gap and Bull Gap, to milepost 368, The Craggy Gardens Picnic Area. Turn left and weave around the mountain to the parking lot. From the parking area it is a half-mile stroll uphill to the rustic shelter at the top.

Craggy Gardens is better known for the June flowering of the native evergreen rhododendron than it is for fall color, but the wooded slopes surrounding the showy "balds" bring fall courting to order. Craggy Gardens and neighboring Craggy Pinnacle provide two of the finest panoramas around because they don't have any trees.

The stroll to Craggy Gardens takes you through maple, beech, and birch woods—in fall a leafy room of yellows, bronze, and orange—to the cobalt blue skies above the field of rhododendron. After wandering through the open meadow invariably rustled up a bit by fall winds, continue past the shelter to the nearby Craggy Gardens visitors center.

From the visitors center parking lot it's a steeper but more rewarding hike to the summit of Craggy Pinnacle, a rugged overlook that offers a commanding view of both sides of the mountain ridge.

The better days in this marvelous place, though, are when fog settles over it, muting the hues and creating a world of dark gray-green mounds and trails that vanish into the mist. There is a magic in monotones of fog that bathes the plants and cloaks the place.

Where the Blue Ridge Parkway winds out of sight to the north, it enters the Asheville Watershed Protection Area, a posted stretch of the road where you must remain in your car. The hardwood forests to the south of the parkway are protected all the way to Black Mountain. It's one of the bright spots along the road.

Continue up the parkway to milepost 355, the turn for Mount Mitchell State Park, which is State 128.

This is your chance to literally top off North Carolina at its first and highest state park. The commanding summit of the 1,677-acre preserve is the highest point east of the Mississippi River, emerging from the middle of the ancient Black Mountains to rise 6,684 feet above sea level. Six peaks of the rugged Black Mountain range are among the ten highest in the East; according to the U.S. Forest Service, eighteen peaks rise more than 6,300 feet above sea level. Yet the range is only fifteen miles long.

Mount Mitchell drips with fog most of the year, and the view from the summit is never guaranteed. The elevation and the cool climate have made the mountain a haven for plants that are normally found in the latitudes of southern Canada. One tree in particular, the Fraser fir, named for early botanist John Fraser, gives the mountain its noteworthy "Nordic" look.

The premier Christmas tree grown commercially in the state, the Fraser fir once thrived on the slopes of Mount Mitchell. In fact, the wood was in such demand that by World War I timber operations threatened to denude the peak, prompting Governor Locke Craig to introduce a bill making Mount Mitchell the first state park, on March 3, 1915.

In the last decade, merely protecting trees from chain saws has not been enough. Today, so many trees are dying that parts of Mount Mitchell look like a ghost forest. Although scientists cannot pin down the exact cause of the accelerating death rate of the Fraser fir and its companion tree the red spruce, evidence indicates a correlation between it and acidic rainfall (some fogs that wash the mountain are as acidic as vinegar). It is theorized that acid rain weakens a tree to the point that it cannot resist natural predators, including the infamous balsam woolly aphid.

Although the tree death is distressing—shocking, if you have not visited the park in ten years or so—it does not diminish the magical quality of hiking the several miles of challenging trails in these woods. The forests are so unusual as to be engaging in spite of their current travails. One trail you must take is the easy three-quarter-mile self-guided Balsam Trail. A guide book is available for fifty cents.

On top of the mountain is an observation tower with metal maps keyed to the horizon so that you can identify surrounding landmarks. Also at the top is the grave of Dr. Elisha Mitchell, namesake explorer who fixed the mountain's supremacy and who died in 1858 from a fall while making a nighttime descent. Mitchell, in conflict with a former student, Thomas Clingman, about the highest peak, had just confirmed his supposition when he fell. Big Tom Wilson who lived in the foothills of the Black Mountains, found Mitchell's body ten days later and carried him out. Because of Wilson's legendary stature, he had a summit in the Black Mountains named after him.

After leaving the Black Mountains, the parkway passage becomes tamer until you reach Buck Creek Gap, the intersection with State 80. Exit the parkway to go north on State 80, but before you do, you might want to take in the overlook, commanding a southern view of the valley just below the parkway.

State 80 west of the parkway is one of the most naturally serene roads in North Carolina. The road passes through Pisgah National Forest in the shadow of the Black Mountain range, paralleling the South Toe River.

The first community you'll see is Busick, offering some promise for collectibles. In the late-nineteenth century, the town was known as Three Forks, named for Three Forks Creek. In fact, three creeks reach a confluence in Busick; two of them have roads that follow the creeks teasingly out of sight from State 80.

Just past Busick is FR 472, a forest service road that winds about two miles to the Black Mountain Campground. This is

Waterfall in the Pisgah National Forest

the gateway to some of the Pisgah National Forest trails that lead to the crest of the Black Mountains, including Mount Mitchell State Park.

There are approximately 25,000 acres in the South Toe River Basin of Pisgah National Forest. Most of the remaining stands of uncut spruce-fir forest, the boreal forest that gives the Black Mountains their dark hue, is between the crest of Black Mountain Ridge and the South Toe River. FR 472 follows the headwaters of the South Toe, eventually intersecting the parkway at Deep Gap, about a five-mile winding crawl from State 80.

There are several trailheads along FR 472. The Mount Mitchell Forest Service Trail, number 190, a 5.6-mile ascent to the summit, begins at the campground. Up and down is a full day hike. Admittedly, to start from here (elevation 3,000 feet) is to take the hard way to the peak, but there are bonuses.

The trail leads near the foundations of historic Camp Alice, once a logging camp, then (as late as the twenties) a lodge for high-country excursions served first by a private rail service and then a motor route.

The details of the Mount Mitchell Trail and several others are on the South Toe River trail map, distributed by the Toecane Ranger District, headquartered in Burnsville, of Pisgah National Forest.

After Black Mountain Campground, State 80 flattens out along the river into a lovely valley. The most noticeable sign of civilization is the Mount Mitchell Golf Course, a public facility in an attractive setting. A part of the complex is the Albert Inn and Lodge.

The forest service is not finished entertaining you just yet, for within two miles is the exit for the Carolina Hemlocks Recreation Area, which includes campgrounds, trailer space, and an improved access to the South Toe River for tubing. It is an infectious treat to drive alongside this campground in warm weather and see the flotillas of inner tubes carry fishbelly white floaters in the clear, cold pool of the South Toe below the campground.

This recreation area is also the trailhead for the Maple Camp Bald Trail and Colbert's Ridge Trail, both of which ascend to the ridge crest of the Black Mountains, looming far above.

State 80 swings to cross the South Toe River as you pass into the community of Hamrick, just west of the wiggle in the river where the recreation area is. The Hamrick Inn is a small bed and breakfast in town. I've not stayed the night, but if rural setting and country roads mean anything, it would have definition here. Notice the occasional cable bridges crossing the South Toe.

En route to Celo, State 80 passes several potteries, craft stores, and a trout pond. Then the road makes a five-mile passage whose majestic setting may be unmatched by any comparable road in the state. South across the fields lofts the peak of Celo Knob (6,326 feet), a magnificent backdrop.

The sign for the P. Mullendorf Recreational Facility is misleading, for although it seems to indicate a public area, in fact it is not. The public access for fishing and swimming is more assured in the U.S. Forest Service facilities.

In Micaville, State 80 merges with US 19E. As you come into town, glimpse to your left to see the post office, housed in an old frame flatiron building. You really can't miss it.

Turn right on US 19E to continue the trip to Spruce Pine. You will pass through Estatoe, an expanding commercial interlude along an otherwise smooth rural passage. The community name legendarily was once that of an Indian princess who drowned herself in a nearby river, which the tribe then named after her. The early white settlers in the region shortened the name to the present-day Toe. Blessedly, the river branches are designated South and North as opposed to left and right.

Downtown Spruce Pine, wouldn't you know, sprawls along the right bank (looking downstream) of the North Toe River. US 19E passes under State 226, the road from the Blue Ridge Parkway; to reach the hub of town, you must turn back south on US 19E business, which is also Oak Street.

I prefer this entrance to Spruce Pine because State 226 through the community of Grassy Creek has become a sort of second "booming" in Spruce Pine, this one of commercial strip development. The first booming began long ago. Spruce Pine is practically the center of Mitchell County's mineral wealth.

This is one of the richest mineral districts in the country, yielding an astonishing fifty-seven different minerals. The most exotic are the gem-quality aquamarine, emerald, tourmaline, and garnet. Less exotic, but more significant to the region's history, are feldspar, mica, and ultrapure quartz.

Put these three facts in your Spruce Pine trivia chest: the 200-inch reflecting mirror in the Mount Palomar telescope was made from local ultrapure quartz; Tiffany's of New York once operated the Crabtree Emerald Mine in nearby Little Switzerland; and, finally, Bon Ami scouring powder used local feldspar, ground to a polishing powder that will not scratch, as its key ingredient.

Mining is old history here. Several sites north of Spruce Pine were worked by Native Americans, presumably for mica, still an important source of mineral wealth. Not much of this underground history is readily visible in downtown Spruce Pine, occurring as it does on State 226 east of town and east of the approach on US 19E.

While still providing a living for many in the community, mining does provide recreation for many more who visit. Before exploring Spruce Pine, you may want to take a short side trip to investigate the area's mining history. Following State 226 south to the Blue Ridge Parkway will take you to the Museum of North Carolina Minerals. A visit will steep you in the geologic lore of Little Switzerland and Spruce Pine and free you up to take your chances at some of the commercial mines nearby, where you may try your luck for a gem or two.

In 1909 the rail line arrived in Spruce Pine—taking advantage of the gentle gradients along the river to negotiate access into the otherwise isolated regions guarded by steep terrain—and Spruce Pine leaped from being a small village to being a town. There are more than a few architectural gems right in the middle of town, but Spruce Pine's pulse is better taken by the river, especially near the 1909 train depot. The Spruce Pine Depot is the oldest building in town, typical of the architecture of the parent railroad line, the Chicago, Cincinnati and Ohio Railroad. Next to the depot is a commemorative plaque honoring the campsite of the Overmountain men, who stopped here on September 28, 1780, on their way to the Battle of Kings Mountain in South Carolina. The name comes from the fact that the men journeyed over the mountains to engage Maj. Patrick Ferguson and his band of Tory troops, who threatened the sanctity of the mountain men's existence. The battle was decisive, killing Ferguson and routing the Tory force.

Enjoy an eye-opening breakfast at the Cedar Crest Restaurant, as enjoyable for the local residents who gather in shifts as it is for the coffee, grits, eggs, and biscuits. Once a department store, the restaurant has very high tin ceilings and ceiling fans.

Flanking the restaurant are numerous stores. One in particular, The Twisted Laurel Gallery, stocks proof of the creative talent that is mineable from these hills. The gallery is open six days a week during summer, weekends the remainder of the year.

The Gunter building, on the corner of Oak and Topaz, was constructed for Charles Gunter in the early 1930s by two local rock masons. These fellows certainly strutted their stuff; notice the patterned rock work fashioned from biotite, the black form of mica. I've never seen a building like it.

The last walking stop is the 400-foot-long footbridge, plainly visible from downtown. It leads to the Pinebridge Inn and Executive Center, which looks suspiciously like a school. . . . It is, indeed, the old Harris School, converted to its present use in the mid-1980s. The site is chiseled into a flattened side of a hill overlooking the river. The rooms are large with high ceilings. The bridge, built in 1929, makes for easy access to the school from downtown.

Although the English Inn is a private residence, it is a Spruce Pine touchstone that you should drive by. From Oak Avenue cross the highway bridge (State 226) and turn right on Greenwood Road. Take the next left, which is English Road, and continue bearing left; the English Inn will be on your right.

Isaac English built a log cabin here (the right-hand component of what looks to be one building) in 1765, and it has been added onto ever since. The house, which is private, now belongs to a family in Tennessee which has owned it since 1929. It was one of the first inns and taverns in the western part of North Carolina; it ceased operating as an inn in the 1930s. There's a lot of lore about the place: the city limits once split the structure; and during the Civil War the owners hid Union troops inside. More significantly for the town, there once stood on the grounds a large hemlock tree that was misidentified as a "spruce pine."

The Penland School of Crafts is the next stop. To get there, return to State 226 and go north through the industrial heart of Spruce Pine toward Bakersville. About three and a half miles north of the light at Oak Avenue and the State 226 bridge, the road will level, dropping to a watercourse. Turn left onto Penland Road (at a small store on the right) and follow the road downstream. After about a mile of loopy driving, turn right into the entrance road to Penland, decidedly uphill.

You'll pass a small school before coming to a turn in front of an imposing building, the Penland Gallery, which is in the old weaving cabin (hardly a cabin anymore). This serves as the visitors center/craft shop for Penland School of Crafts, a name that is synonymous with fine handcrafted work.

Just beyond the visitors center is the meadow, overlooked by the lodge and the dining hall. This genuine, if very rural, campus is a simply inspiring setting.

A weaver in Penland

Penland is more than sixty years old, founded by Miss Lucy Morgan, who came to Mitchell County to help her brother run the Appalachian School, a boarding and elementary school sponsored by the Episcopal Church.

Miss Morgan sought to revive the art of handweaving. Initially the women wove at home, but eventually volunteer labor and donated materials constructed the present Weaving Building.

Instructors were brought in and other handcrafts were produced, glass items in particular. The reputation for good instruction, and an environment conducive to concentration and fostering a closeness with the surroundings, vaulted Penland to the pinnacle of craft instructional centers. Since its founding, it has grown to 450 acres and forty-seven buildings. Many studios have been added, and there are more than 100 full-time craftspeople on staff.

This is a place where art shakes hands with craft—while the emphasis is on function, some of the items are simply too beautiful to use. It's a treat to walk in; the creativity is stunning. Each year there is a lengthy schedule of instructors and courses available through the summer. Anyone can apply to be a Penland Fellow, but the typically two-week sessions are not inexpensive and the student must also pay room and board. The Visitors Center houses the work of many Penland artisans and is open year-round, Monday through Saturday, 10:00 A.M. to 12:00 P.M. and 1:00 P.M. to 4:30 P.M.; Sunday 12:00 P.M. to 4:30 P.M.

To continue on toward Bakersville, return to State 226, and turn north. It is an unhurriable route, remarkable for the few houses along the way. If you sense you are remote, it is true; the crenellated geography of Mitchell County keeps it rural. Bakersville, the seat of Mitchell County, is in the flats beside Cane Creek.

The U.S. Forest Service has a small office here in the municipal-looking building on your left as you approach "main street" in Bakersville, which is the junction of State 226 and Mitchell Avenue. Turn left on Roan View Drive and park; the forest service office is downstairs in the first building on the right. You can pick up some guide maps to Roan Mountain and the trails in this district of Pisgah National Forest.

To get to Roan Mountain, follow State 226 to the next intersection of State 261. At the intersection of State 226, which breaks off to the left, and State 261, you'll see the small wood-frame McBee Building, one of the oldest structures standing in Bakersville. From here, follow the signs to Roan Mountain. It is only twelve miles, but the trip will take at least thirty minutes on the serpentine road—a marvelous introduction to a remote and beautiful region.

In about six miles, approximately halfway to Roan Mountain, you'll come to the crossroads community of Glen Ayre, with, among other things, two red barns in the valley. It's a peaceful place, once called Brighton, sitting on flat land carved out by Little Rock Creek, which is joined by Little Green Creek.

You'll see an abandoned school that has been converted to a nursery. Then State 261 sidles along the creek before beginning a series of switchback turns marking the ascent to Carvers Gap. As you climb, you will notice how the tree cover begins to thin out, until there is only brushy growth on the steep hillsides—some trees, but certainly not a forest.

Try to imagine what this road is like during the last two weeks in June, when more than 10,000 visitors a day make their way to Roan Mountain to see the native Catawba rhododendron bloom. Imagine the migration during the time both Tennessee and North Carolina hold their annual Rhododendron Festival.

It's sort of a rite of passage in these airy elevations to put your blinders on and make the pilgrimage to what is one of the largest natural rhododendron gardens in the world. These are natural gardens; no human designed the wonderful expanses. The place breathes grandeur any time of the year; in the last part of June, it duns the senses. For the record (and the bragging rights), the majority of the rhododendron gardens are in North Carolina, not Tennessee.

At Carvers Gap, which straddles the state line, North Carolina's State 261 becomes Tennessee's State 143. The gap is the low spot between Roan Mountain, to the southwest, and Round Bald, part of the thirteen miles of associated summits considered the Roan Mountain Massive, immediately north-

The Craggys, The Blacks, and the Highlands of Roan

east. The gap is where you make up your mind what you want to do next.

There is some pullover parking, but the most obvious thing to do is to make the left turn onto the forest service spur road. This leads south, ascending to the rhododendron gardens, where there is a visitors center, rest rooms, and a handicapped trail.

Your statehood can be in question quickly here as well since North Carolina nudges neighboring Tennessee somewhere in the gap.

Park at the end of the parking lot and walk into the grassy meadow; you may in fact follow what seems to be an old roadbed leading from the parking lot. It was indeed the carriage route for a remarkable hostelry. You will see some granite piers in the meadow, part of the foundation of the Cloudland Hotel, constructed by John Thomas Wilder in 1885. Imagine a 166-room hotel commanding a view of the valley to the south and west.

Wilder promoted the hotel vigorously, citing not only the breezes and cool temperatures but such oddities as the "circular rainbows" visible on the north side of the mountain after storms, and also the "mountain music," an indeterminate sound attributed to the highly charged air of these peaks. If you get the feeling this is no place to be in a lightning storm, you're right. Ironically, there might be no place better to watch a storm sweep up the valley below.

One of the drawbacks of the Cloudland Hotel was getting there; it was an arduous stage ride from Johnson City. Eventually the hotel was closed and the mountain was timbered.

Today, the Appalachian Trail sneaks up on the far side of the Cloudland site, and inevitably there are hikers and backpackers passing through, heading north or south. There is a spur trail leading from the Cloudland site to Roan High Bluff.

To see the rhododendron gardens, drive to the next parking area and turn out. There will be a small shelter and several paved trails leading south through the 600-acre rhododendron gardens that have made Roan Mountain so renowned. Notice, too, the tree cover—all red spruce and Fraser fir; this is the natural forest cover of this very high elevation.

The paved trails loop down the southwest face of the mountain, which is clad almost exclusively in Catawba rhododendron, a plant named by John Fraser.

The Catawba rhododendron prefers the typically cool and moist atmosphere that washes high mountaintops. *Rhododendron catawbiense*, as botanists know it, couldn't be happier than when it's wrapped in fog. That happens more often than not, as regular visitors can verify. Even if you miss the rhododendron bloom, you can walk in a portion of natural landscape so rare that it is not duplicated in scale anywhere else in the uppermost reaches of the mountains.

From the trails at the parking areas of the gardens, you can see scattered evergreen trees—pyramidal red spruce and Fraser fir—punctuating the fringes of the rounded rhododendron plants. Other than the rare green alder, few other shrubby plants share the 600-acre site with the rhododendrons. This paucity of plant species is unusual, unique at this scale, and ecologically unexplained, though it has been documented in European settlement records and noted in Native American lore. To the best knowledge of scientists, Roan Mountain has been dominated by a single shrub perhaps since the last glacial epoch.

It is no less amazing to walk in the spongy soil today. The various habitats are so unusual and unexpected that it is easy to see what enthralled these astute observers of earlier centuries.

Botanists call the gardens a "shrub bald." The term *bald* is a descriptive term for any of several mountaintop plant associations in the Southern Appalachians that are characteristi-

The Craggys, The Blacks, and the Highlands of Roan

cally, and sometimes mysteriously, treeless. In nature's order of natural succession followed elsewhere in the mountains, trees ultimately will reforest a clearing. Not so on the shrub balds and the adjoining grassy balds along the Roan Mountain Massive. For various reasons, the balds remain bald.

After enjoying the loop tour, or the self-guided tour, strike out at the end of the westernmost parking lot to Roan High Bluff, elevation 6,287 feet, for a commanding view of the valleys below. Then return to Carvers Gap and park.

While the grassy bald before you doesn't appear nearly as remarkable as the spectacular gardens you just left, the visual simplicity masks a botanical richness.

According to the U.S. Forest Service, there are more rare and endangered species found on Roan Mountain Massif than in any other location in the southern Appalachian Mountains. Massif is the term used to describe the immense ridge of Roan, on both sides of Carvers Gap.

These hills have been scoured and gleaned by a "who's who" of historic botanical figures, among them André Michaux, who journeyed here from France via Charleston in the eighteenth century, and Dr. Asa Gray, who declared it "the most beautiful mountain east of the Rocky Mountains" in the late nineteenth century.

The Appalachian Trail sidles through or over a stile (there are two styles of stiles) to ascend the summit of Round Bald, the first of nearly nine miles of grassy balds (mostly treeless mountaintops) aligning northeast-southwest from the gap. Round Bald looks like a big grassy meadow from below because it is, although close to the gap are a few scattered rhododendron and even Fraser fir. There's a small group of Fraser fir nearly on the summit, something to shoot for as you huff to 5,826 feet. When you reach the trees, you are on top of the world: that's the only way to describe the feeling.

The trail beckons north, to a still higher bald, named for Jane. Then it continues, topping Grassy Ridge Bald and Little Hump Mountain, down to Bradley Gap and up again to Hump Mountain, the grass-clad end. But it's not all grass; some grassy-looking plants are sedges. The closer you look at the earth, the more differences you will see. Each mile seems to boast its own particular mix of plants.

Although nearly all the balds were used as horse or cattle pasture for some of their modern history, these animals are not allowed today. But goats are. These hoofed ruminants are browsers, and because of their eating preferences, they have become a viable management technique of the forest service.

Goats love blackberry plants and blackberry plants love the sunny, grassy ridge tops. So when you follow the white blazes of the Appalachian Trail to the summit of Round Bald, past the exquisite tuft of trees on top, you will find a sign that reads: "These open balds provide a unique home for sensitive plants. Blackberries and hawthorns are threatening to take over the bald areas and reduce the habitat for sensitive plants. We [U.S. Forest Service] are conducting research to see if goats can protect the sensitive plant habitat."

The hero of the grassy highlands may indeed turn out to be the goat. If you have to share a few moments on the top of the world watching the wind rippling the grasses, and the cloud shadows marching over the mountainsides below, what better company than a nonmotorized mower that's helping to keep it that way?

This is the end of the tour. You may reverse your route to return to Spruce Pine, or continue on Tennessee 143 north through Roan Mountain State Park to the town of Roan Mountain, Tennessee, which is on US 19E, and follow that road back to Spruce Pine.

In the Area

Folk Art Center (Asheville): 704-298-7928

Blue Ridge Parkway (Asheville): 704-259-0701

Mount Mitchell State Park: 704-675-4611

Mitchell Area Chamber of Commerce (Spruce Pine): 800-227-3912 or 704-765-9483

Pisgah National Forest (Asheville): 704-257-4200

Toecane Ranger District (Burnsville): 704-682-6146

Cedar Crest Restaurant (Spruce Pine): 704-765-6124

The Twisted Laurel Gallery (Spruce Pine): 704-765-1562

Pinebridge Inn and Executive Center (Spruce Pine): 704-765-5543

Penland Visitors Center (Penland): 704-765-6211

Roan Mountain State Park (Roan Mountain, Tennessee): 615-772-3303

2 ~ The Ski Country Without Snow

From Hickory take US 321 north to Boone. Head west on US 421/321 to Vilas. Take State 194 west to Banner Elk, then State 184 to State 105 back to Boone.

Highlights: *The Blowing Rock; the Annie Cannon Memorial Gardens and Broyhill Park; Appalachian Ski Mountain; the Tweetsie Railroad and Theme Park; Boone,* Horn in the West, *the oldest outdoor drama about the Revolutionary War, and also the Appalachian Cultural Museum; the Mast Store; and the Valle Crucis Episcopal Church Conference Center.*

This tour is a loop starting at Blowing Rock through Boone to Banner Elk and back, roads that are normally traveled by cars with skis strapped on top and skiers bundled inside. The trip requires at least one overnight stay, with two days on the road. Accommodations are abundant and usually easily obtained except for peak fall color weekends.

The roads that thread this isolated region, wandering through secluded valleys and decidedly rumpled countryside, lead to places where time itself seems pleasantly poised in a long-past era. What you measure as miles on a

The Ski Country Without Snow

map might as well be a journey of decades—and, in fact, can take a lot longer than it would in flatter country.

Blowing Rock is one of the older mountain resort communities, incorporated in 1889, although folks had been summering there for many years before that. The town retains the small-scale charm of a turn-of-the-century resort. It's quaint, almost quirky, and has an easygoing air about it.

The Blowing Rock, a rock promontory slightly down the mountain from the town, juts dramatically toward a commanding view of the John's River Valley below. This is one of the oldest private pay-for-the-view tourist attractions, identifiable by the rustic lodge/gift shop that has the view fenced off from the parking lot. The dated exterior of the building cannot take away from the spectacle on the other side of the turnstile.

The uplifting wind currents from the valley have been known to blow light objects back to those who throw them off the rock (or what is now the observation deck), hence the town's name. Indian legend, however, states that the benevolent winds returned a lovesick Chickasaw warrior who so lamented leaving his Cherokee lover that he leaped from the rock. That may have worked once, but . . .

Anyway, around these lofting, cooling winds developed this summer respite, a development certainly feeding off the ambition of Hugh MacRae, who at the same time (1890s) was developing Linville and Grandfather Mountain.

Blowing Rock immediately defuses any preconceptions you might have about high-impact summer places. What makes it nice is there's not a lot of there, there. (Thank you, Gertrude Stein.) Contributing to the personable nature of the community is the large number of ma and pa motels and vintage one-story motor courts, typically operated by either resident owners or seasonal operators who live here from April through October.

You might choose a small place such as The Homestead Inn on Morris Street. Staying here is come and go as you please, and you don't feel as though you have to lock your room.

Around the corner on Main Street is Sonny's Grill, the local place for a down-home, good-morning breakfast. The restaurant is no bigger than a dining room and is festooned with Sonny's attitude and witticisms, such as, "I'll tell you why I came home last night drunk. . . . I ran out of money."

Sonny's won't break you, and you'll start the day full.

If you have time for a little walk, head down Laurel Lane to the Annie Cannon Memorial Gardens and Broyhill Park. These civic projects honor the individuals and the centennial of the city. The Glen Burney Trail is a 1.5-mile switchback following New Year's Creek; it begins at the Annie Cannon Memorial Gardens, which contain native plants. Across the road from the trailhead is the more ornate Broyhill Park, a fine place for a lakeside stroll.

You might also enjoy stepping into the Cosmic Coffee House, occupying a 1918 stone building that was once a hardware store, then a filling station. The stone facade is typical of early Blowing Rock architecture. You'll also see it in the Rumple Presbyterian Church and St. Mary's of the Hills Episcopal Church, both on Main Street.

Leave Blowing Rock by way of Main Street and continue on US 321 north, under the Blue Ridge Parkway, toward Boone. From November to February, you can follow the ski-topped cars that turn left quickly on SR 1539 just after passing under the parkway. This road leads to Appalachian Ski Mountain, the oldest ski resort in the Southeast, renowned for its instruction and the variety of ski runs tailored to beginners and intermediate skiers.

The seven-mile stretch of US 321 between Blowing Rock and Boone is busy with attractions and shopping. The two

The Ski Country Without Snow

most well known are Mystery Hill, with its Blue Ridge Heritage Museum, and the Tweetsie Railroad & Theme Park, which is one of the longer running attractions in the state. Seeing Tweetsie can easily take three to five hours, with a gentle type of made-for-little-kids entertainment that, in this video era, seems delightfully down to earth.

Boone, the largest city in the area, is the home of Appalachian University. Since 1952, it has hosted the seasonal outdoor, oldest Revolutionary War drama, the *Horn in the West*. There's no shortage of shopping available as you drive into town.

The old part of this 1871 city lies along US 421, the primary east-west highway. Boone traffic can be tedious, but it doesn't last long.

A suggested stop is the unusual Appalachian Cultural Museum in University Hall, on the east side of US 321. As you enter Boone from Blowing Rock, look on your right for Greene's Motel; turn right just past the motel and just before the Scotchman service station. The museum is on the first floor of University Hall, which is at the top of this drive. Park in the lot to the right.

The museum documents the many cultures that thrived in the isolating geography of the mountains, from pre-European settlements through cultural legacies from as recent as the late 1970s. It tips its hat to the independent nature of the people. An audiovisual show provides the introduction.

The haunting melody of "The Unclouded Day," a traditional family reunion hymn sung by Mary Greene, plays while you meet the families of the mountains in a series of projected images: the work crew who built the Green Park Inn; a baseball team; a Civil War veterans reunion; a hog killing. The pictures offer a private viewing from family albums dating from 1870 to the 1930s.

The remainder of the museum is a collection of artifacts, handsomely displayed, that depict a story of mountain life through the tools and toys of its people. There's a broom made from one piece of wood; photographs of mountaineer/ geologist Elisha Mitchell and his student Thomas Clingman, and a barometer of the type these great geologists used to calibrate the heights of mountains.

There is a collection of looms, and one of the two remaining original Blue Ridge Parkway signs. The eclectic nature of the displays paints a powerful portrait of mountain life. Some things are truly cultural artifacts, such as portions of the yellow brick road and the tin man's suit from the Land of Oz, at one time one of the most popular theme parks in the nation, but gone now. The last room in the museum is a tribute to North Wilkesboro's Junior Johnson, Tom Wolfe's subject in the essay *The Last American Hero*. It's a room filled with two race cars.

Leave the museum, turn right on US 321, and continue into downtown, passing some of the buildings of Appalachian University, and continuing past the Dan'l Boone Inn, famed for its family-style serving of country cooking. Turn left at the junction of US 421 and drive into the older commercial center of Boone. The street flares slightly wider for parking, and the buildings on the north side of the road seem to be notched into the hillside. This part of the city is stamped with the mood of a different era. One store you may notice is the Mast General Store. Don't stop here now; you're going to the real thing ten miles ahead.

Continue on US 421/321 out of Boone, driving west, to the community of Vilas. Turn left (south) on State 194. If you haven't buckled up your seat belt, do so; a sign at the turn warns that vehicles more than a certain length will have difficulty on this road, and it's true. Although you're traveling only four miles, you'll wish the car had a hinge in the middle.

The Ski Country Without Snow

The road climbs, then winds beside Baird Creek and houses very close to the road. It follows the creek to the confluence with the Watauga River, which it crosses. Here, the views of an absolutely lovely valley unfold, seen past a barn noticeable because of the chevron planking. The road hugs the western rim of the basin, past farms along the valley floor.

You've just wound your way back into Valle Crucis, the valley of the cross, where the dominant enterprise, and one of the friendliest neighbors, is the Mast Store, which will be on your left. By the time you step past the wooden door bearing the plaque of the National Register of Historic Places, you are more than aware that ten miles looks like ten decades. Since 1882, it has been the business of the Mast Store to save valley residents a trip to town, which once took considerably longer than the drive you just completed.

The Mast Store can still save you the trip. The shelves have everything you could possibly need (or imagine you need) for life in the last century—and most of this one. It is a post office, produce outlet, hardware store, and dry goods supplier. There are hog rings, cowbells, patent medicines, boots, coveralls, eggs, honey, cast-iron skillets, and sunbonnets handmade by a valley resident. There is a full display of colorful speckled enamelware.

If a bolt drops off your tractor on the drive up the valley, you can look in the burnished octagon bolt bins for a replacement. These utilitarian furnishings are museum pieces in their own right.

There is a woodstove, rocking chairs, and a checkerboard where bottle caps are the playing pieces. There is no limit on playing, staying, or gawking. It's a good thing, too: the Mast Store is where the city now comes to the country.

General Manager Tracy Parris remembers the early days of his twenty-two-year history with the store. "I started sweeping floors for Mr. Mast when I was ten years old," states Parris, "and there wasn't any tourism here twenty years ago. This was just a local store."

The charm of the place is just that. The doors open at 6:30 A.M. to get the mail up and close at 6:30 P.M. six days a week. (Sunday hours are 1 to 6 P.M.) By 8:30 A.M., you can learn everything you need to know for the day by hanging around the stove, even in summer.

In 1883, W. W. Mast purchased half interest in the store from founder Henry Taylor, a year after construction. In 1913, Mast bought out Taylor, and for sixty years his family built the reputation of the store that "carries everything from cradles to caskets."

You should climb to the second story of the central section of the three-part building to see an actual rope-handled coffin. A coffin like this is the last purchase for many Valle Crucis residents.

In 1979, John and Fay Cooper purchased the store and started reaching beyond the valley with their merchandise and down-home appeal. Sales boomed, the store grew, and Cooper opened The Annex, a 1909 vintage store, a quarter mile down the road. The Annex offers quality apparel for all seasons downstairs, and outdoor clothing and equipment, including hand-tied trout flies, upstairs.

Physically attached to The Annex, but independently owned and operated, is a small shop known as The Candy Barrel, featuring more than 700 candy varieties.

In 1989, the store expanded again, moving and refurbishing the 1907 Little Red School House, which many Valle Crucis residents attended. The school is now located behind the main store and sells educational toys.

Although the store works hard at mingling a period atmosphere with modern retail reality, the times, they are a-changing, a little bit anyway.

The Mast Store

"I ordered cast-iron cookware from the Atlanta Stove Works," recalls Tracy Parris, "and after 110 years, they went out of business. I couldn't believe it."

So he found another supplier, because he says that nothing lasts like cast-iron cookware, and anything newer wouldn't sell or, perhaps worse, would look out of place here.

If you drive a quarter mile past The Annex, you'll come to the Mast Farm Inn, a recently restored Mast family home that has been renovated as a bed and breakfast. The view from the front porch is easy on the eyes, offering the broad sweep of the Watauga River Valley.

Return to State 194 and turn left (west) onto it to enter one of the most beautiful parts of the valley. The road plunges into the woods and follows Dutch Creek for a mile, then passes an elegant farmhouse on the right: The Inn at the Taylor House is a luxurious bed and breakfast.

It's about as tranquil a setting as you'll find, poised opposite the confluence of Dutch and Clark's Creeks and on the verge of a small highland valley. I haven't stayed here, but I have toured the rooms, which are elegantly furnished. It is an upscale getaway for the owners, Chip and Roland Schwab, who also co-own (with Heinz Schwab) Atlanta's Hedgerose Heights Inn.

Leaving the 1911 farmhouse the winding road ascends above the valley floor on the north side. After rounding a bend, you suddenly see what appears to be a dormitory or large school. That's a good guess; it's an Episcopal Church conference center, and its history figures in the history of Valle Crucis. So does the history of the wonderful stone church nearby, the Church of the Holy Cross.

The Episcopal presence began here in 1842 with the Right Reverend Levi Ives, the Bishop of North Carolina. He, in fact, climbed a nearby ridge and interpreted the pattern of stream

The Ski Country Without Snow

confluence in the valley below him to form a St. Andrews Cross, which looks like a plus sign doing a cartwheel. The valley he saw is supposedly the one below, but the exact location of the viewing, as well as the alteration of the creek alignments in a century and a half, have clouded the details. Undoubtedly, Bishop Ives gave the region the inspired Latin name that means "vale of the cross."

Bishop Ives established the Society of the Holy Cross, the first monastic order in the Anglican Communion since the 1500s. The small log cabin adjacent to the church is the only building surviving from that era.

The monastic order disbanded in 1852; the ministry in the valley flagged as well until 1895, when Bishop Joseph Blount Cheshire visited, seeking to revive the presence of the church. By the early twentieth century, Bishop Junius Horner of the newly established Missionary District of Asheville had fashioned a community around the church, constructing the building that served as a school for grades one through twelve. In 1925, the present church was built, with its native stone exterior and exquisite interior with unusual wainscoting, roof trusses, and a unique floor tiled with end cuts of hardwood blocks. The congregation is still active today.

Leave the church and climb the several switchbacks out of the valley; there are houses so close to the road that I would not want to live in them in snowy weather. There is one superlative overlook—a wide spot above the valley before the road moves back into the woods—where you can pull over and view this serene, secluded place, although this stop is more easily made on a return visit than when heading west on State 194 as you are now.

The road does eventually crest the ridge, slithering along the side of one watershed to poke its nose through to the side of another. This all happens in less than six miles. Suddenly the road levels out and you are easing into Banner Elk, a town

Ferns, wild geraniums, Clinton's lily, and mayapples

named for the Banner family, who lived on the nearby Elk River.

In 1900, the Reverend Edgar Tufts, a Presbyterian minister, founded Lees-McRae College, which was named for teacher Elizabeth McRae and benefactor Mrs. S. P. Lees. Tufts, however, was the prime benefactor of the town, establishing the Cannon Memorial Hospital and the Grandfather Home for Children, institutions that have been indispensable in shaping the character of the community.

Continue through town and turn north on State 184, which will carry you up and over Beech Mountain (well,

The Ski Country Without Snow

almost—the road crosses at 5,000 feet) before a descent into the Beech Mountain Resort Ski Area and parking lot. The view is worth the drive any time of year.

Return to downtown Banner Elk and turn south on State 184. Gabriell's, the restaurant on the corner of State 194 and State 184, is a place for a hot cup of coffee or to try Italian cuisine. Next door (and connected) is Elly's Baked Goods, if you need something to keep you going on the road home.

Leave Banner Elk on State 184, which winds past the entrance to Sugar Mountain Ski Resort on the west side of the highway. Then turn left on State 105 almost directly opposite Grandfather Mountain, and pass the entrance to Seven Devils and Hawks Nest Ski Areas and Hounds Ears. After twelve miles you will come to the junction with US 321 in Boone. Turn right (south) to return to Blowing Rock.

In the Area

The Blowing Rock (Blowing Rock): 704-295-7111

The Homestead Inn (Blowing Rock): 704-295-9559

Sonny's Grill (Blowing Rock): 704-295-7577

Appalachian Ski Mountain: 704-295-7828

Appalachian Cultural Museum (Boone): 704-262-3117

Horn in the West (Boone): 704-264-2120

Dan'l Boone Inn (Boone): 704-264-8657

Mystery Hill (Blowing Rock): 704-264-2792

Tweetsie Railroad & Theme Park, 704-264-9061

The Mast Store (Valle Crucis): 704-963-6511

The Inn at the Taylor House (Valle Crucis): 704-963-5581

Gabriell's (Banner Elk): 704-898-7558

North Carolina High Country Host (accommodations information): 800-438-7500 or 704-264-1299

3 ~ New River Christmas Tree Country

From Winston-Salem follow US 421 west to I-77 north to US 21 north outside of Elkin. Ascend to the Blue Ridge Parkway past Roaring Gap. Follow the parkway south to Glendale Springs. Head north on US 221 to Jefferson, then take State 88 south toward Sparta.

Highlights: *Stone Mountain State Park; the Blue Ridge Parkway; open artists' studios in West Jefferson; canoe rentals on the New River; a North Carolina State University agricultural experimental farm; and Alleghany County's Choose and Cut Weekend.*

This tour is a freewheeling loop through the northwest counties of the state. You have to get on the Blue Ridge Parkway before you begin the loop. The trip is drivable in one day, but that would be a "been there done that" tour. You could see it but not savor it. I recommend repeated day trips.

I have driven portions of this tour at least once a year every year since the mid–1960s, loving every repeated mile, a combination of a completely, continually enriching experience and the acknowledgment that the place is a touchstone.

This tour begins on US 21 north of Elkin, ascending the Blue Ridge Mountains to Roaring Gap. There are two winding ribbons here, depending on whether you travel by car or canoe. The Blue Ridge Parkway, which runs northeast to southwest through Alleghany, Wilkes, and Ashe Counties, is at its scenic peak along this loop. The ancient New River, flowing southwest to northeast, from Watauga County to Virginia, meanders through here in a bewildering series of coils. Each mode of transportation has a guide book's worth of sights and opportunities. This tour puts you in the right playground; you have to make your game from a multitude of attractions.

The New River will be all around you, but it can be very hard to see. The most exquisite of all views are those of the stained-glass land patterns of the well-tended farms. From parkway elevations, the vistas embrace Grant Wood landscapes. If you've never swayed through these winding mountain roads, you'll find them easy on the eyes, gentle on the mind, and soothing to the soul.

This is a tour for late April to mid November, to catch the best these hills offer. Even in the dead of summer, the temperature will be ten degrees lower than in the city.

Fall colors in these parts may linger well beyond mid-October, and the range is spectacular, particularly along the Blue Ridge Parkway. Because this is a popular tourist destination in fall, I suggest making reservations for any overnight accommodations needed in October before the end of June.

On a clear fall day, you can see the houses of Roaring Gap in the far distance as you follow the US 21 bypass around Elkin. The houses perch on the edge of the mountain, and by the time you pass through State Road to Thurmond, the crown of the hill hides them from view.

One mile past Thurmond, on the west side of US 21, is a brown state park sign noting Stone Mountain. The exit is onto Traphill Road, so named because one man regularly set up wild turkey traps on a hill near the outskirts of town.

The park preserves a local landmark and the surrounding countryside. Stone Mountain is a 600-million-year-old granite pluton, which means a big rock blister mountain: it formed underground as a liquid rock intrusion and cooled to become a granitic gumdrop, which considerable erosion exposed.

Fall weekends have traffic jams, but what a splendid place to slow-crawl on country roads. This is a magnificent park, with free-flowing streams and campsites along them, a 200-foot waterfall, the 600-foot-high wall of the mountain, and more than 13,000 acres bordering the Blue Ridge Parkway. Rock climbing is permitted in the park, making for high spectator drama. The climbing routes are easy to find and bolted for safety. The summit, a challenging ascent, offers unobstructed views of the surrounding hills and a chance to see the weathered "moonscape" surface of the exposed rock.

Raccoons enjoy the park, too

Hiking to the top of the mountain and the return trip is a half-day jaunt if you are in excellent shape. Be sure to carry a canteen if you go; there's no water on the top, and the climb will leave you breathless from exhilaration and exertion.

Continuing north on US 21, immediately on the left is one of the loveliest homes of the small community of Doughton, at the headwaters of the Elkin River. Directly ahead on top of the mountain you may still catch a glimpse of perched homes. Most likely, as the road winds in its ascent, you'll see the clear-cut of a timbering operation.

On your left, on the downhill side of the highway, the roadbed of old US 21 is visible. The road you are on more closely follows the grade of an old railroad that once carried people up the mountain.

Where the timber hasn't been cut, the road is a passage through a high cove forest whose dominant trees are tulip poplar, hickory, and oak. In fall, the tulip poplars remind me of paint brushes dipped in butter yellow paint and standing on end.

You'll find one superb scenic overlook on US 21; stop and take a gasp. Below you is the broad, flat plain of Happy Valley, the drainage basin framed by the Blue Ridge Mountains (where you are) and the Brushy Mountains, the horizon due south. On a clear day, you can see the Sauratown Mountains with the clearly identifiable knob of Pilot Mountain dominating the vista. Winston-Salem's tallest buildings, some seventy miles away, are sometimes visible. Turning back to the west, you can see the edge of the Blue Ridge escarpment and the flat top of Table Mountain near Morganton.

The ascent steepens and makes one last sharp right turn before slowing its wind into Roaring Gap. The gap is one of the first available places to cross over the escarpment of the Blue Ridge. This is also the eastern Continental Divide, elevation 2,972 feet above sea level. South of the gap, water flows to the Atlantic; on the other side of the gap, which is just past the Roaring Gap Post Office, water drains to the Mississippi by way of the New River.

There has always been a post office in Roaring Gap in the low building on the left, but in thirty years the other buildings have seen a variety of uses. The single building to the left has been a dry goods store, an antique store, and even a restaurant. The larger building was once a service station/store with the post office. All of these conveniences served primarily the summer visitors of the more than 200 families of Roaring Gap.

Turn right into Roaring Gap, a private summer residential community established by Alexander Chatham of Elkin in 1890. The entrance descends into a beautiful cove forest, and within two-tenths of a mile crosses the small stream and headwaters of the lake, which will be on your left. On your right are the grounds of what was once a YMCA camp. Be mindful of your speed; many curves are blind and there are bridle paths that cross the development.

When you come to an intersection, continue straight. After driving past Doughton View Road (the houses have a view of Doughton at the foot of the mountain), you'll see the woods yield to a golf course. Some of the houses on the south side of the road, hidden behind tremendous white pine trees, are among those visible from US 21 as the road begins to ascend the mountain.

Most of the homes were built in the early twentieth century and echo the resort architecture of the private homes in Pinehurst. You will see one architectural feature that dates some of the homes; it is bark siding. The bark and wood of the American chestnut are extraordinarily durable materials, with a natural rot resistance that is unmatched by other woods. A blight killed the American chestnut during the 1930s, eliminating the tree as a source of building materials and fixing the latest decade that the houses you see were probably built.

You'll pass the golf club on the right and come to the intersection of Laurel Drive; directly ahead is the Gothic Revival Roaring Gap Chapel.

Continue to the right, past several homes, until you see the great lawn of the Roaring Gap Inn, which was operating as a hostelry as late as the early 1970s. Below the inn on the south side of the road are several cottages that were once part of its operation. In its glory days, the Roaring Gap Inn was the seat of entertainment and dining for members and guests of Roaring Gap.

The road loops around the inn and past several tennis courts and some very expansive houses, hemmed in by rhododendron and sheared hemlock hedges.

Once around the club, take your first right turn and drive through the interior of the forest that returns to the chapel, then turn right on Laurel Drive. Ignore the turn to the community center and follow Laurel Drive into the woods past the stables, which will be above the road on the right.

The most remarkable house in the development is on the right, with some peculiar concrete walks and tanks leading up to it. For many years, this was a U. S. Fish and Wildlife Service fish hatchery. It was abandoned in the late seventies and has been converted into a private residence.

Continue straight, bearing left around the lake, noting how the small boathouses and bathhouses on the lake reflect an earlier era. The lake and its several shingled houses and boathouses make a watercolor composition waiting for an artist. There are wonderful dated touches, such as rock walls, quartz rock chimneys, and gourd purple martin houses.

Return to US 21, turn right, and drive about one and a half miles, past the entrance to Old Beau Golf Course and Country Club, past the charming Antioch Church on the right, The High Meadows Inn (a small hotel with modestly priced rooms), the golf course of High Meadows Country

Club, to Camp Cheerio Road. Turn left. On your left will be Pine Shadows Farm, the largest choose and cut Christmas tree farm in Alleghany County and one of the top tree growers in the state. It's managed and worked by Alfred Motsinger with assistant manager Andy Royall.

The farm is a seasonally happy spot any time of year, but it takes a lot of hard work to make it—and all other tree farms—a successful plantation. The average-sized Christmas tree is nearly fifteen years old, and it doesn't become manicured without some tender loving cultivation. Growers cut as many as six million trees per season. More than 5,000 acres of tree farms in Alleghany County contribute to that total.

The most desirable tree species is the Fraser fir, native to the highest elevations of North Carolina and Tennessee, named after pioneering botanist John Fraser. It has flat, smooth needles with rounded tips; it is soft and fragrant, and it retains its needles remarkably long after cutting.

Fraser fir prefers high, cool climates and well-drained soil, virtually a geographic description of the hilly terrain of Alleghany, Ashe, and Watauga Counties, the New River country.

A tree grower's year begins in late February and early March, readying ground for new seedlings. When growth starts, the all-important "top" work begins, seeing that the tree has one dominant leader and that the lateral branches extend uniformly from the tree, which sets its future shape.

Alfred and Andy do it all at Pine Shadows Farm, from planting to cutting. Two years ago, they selected five trees they liked and won three state awards: the Fraser fir was both the best of its class and the overall Grand Champion, earning the farm the right to represent North Carolina in the 1994 National Christmas Tree Association competition.

You may be early to choose your tree, but Pine Shadows also offers reasonably priced landscape plants (hemlock, rhododendron, mountain laurel, and other mountain species) for sale in easily moveable, affordable sizes.

Continue climbing Camp Cheerio Road to the first intersection and turn right. Continue across a small creek to a stop sign.

By the way, if you are looking for seasonal decorations, the fence on the left side of the road is typically covered with tangles of bittersweet vine (*Celastrus scandens*). The multicolored fruit (yellow husk, orange berry) is attractive, although the vine is insidiously invasive.

At the stop sign turn left; at the next intersection turn left again on Rash Road. Follow this to the Blue Ridge Parkway and turn left (south) to begin an incredibly memorable drive— one of the best along the parkway.

Before you go, you may want to grab a bite at Mountain Hearth Lodge and Restaurant, located just off the parkway. To reach the restaurant, after your left turn onto the parkway, drive about a mile to turn left on Bull Head Road (SR 1109), the first paved road near milepost 231. The restaurant is on the south side of the parkway. You can make reservations for dinner or for a room. The cuisine is innovative American café style. Return to the parkway and continue south.

The fall color along this section of the Blue Ridge Parkway, from the Virginia state line to Blowing Rock, North Carolina, is typically the most varied in hue, and reliable for a show year after year. Look for the foliage to peak between mid-October and Halloween. The most vivid hues are from the tree planted to shade the farms, the sugar maple. The tree occurring naturally by the roadside, the pumpkin-colored sassafras, and the golden yellow chinquapin oak and hickory augment the show.

Drive south, past the overlooks of Stone Mountain and Devil's Garden, until the parkway swings through a notch in

New River Christmas Tree Country

the escarpment at Mahogany Rock to overlook the pristine farm community of Glade Valley.

Every year, a magnificent mountain ash bedecked and bejeweled with fist-sized clusters of orange-red fruit spreads above the parkway at one location: it is a ritual sighting.

Continue your southerly course to enter Doughton Park (milepost 238), the largest recreation area along this scenic road. It has multiple campsites and a small lodge for overnight stays. Have your camera ready for stops such as Brinegar's Cabin (milepost 238.5).

In fact, park at the cabin and ascend to a clearing above the parking lot where wildflowers become perches for passing butterflies—monarchs, viceroys, and tiger swallowtails—flitting their way south.

If you want a hike to the "top of the world," turn in at the sign for The Bluffs Lodge, then turn right again to the parking area where the road loops to reverse back. Climb north to the highest place you see—it's quite a view and very peaceful. On your way back to the parkway, turn right to pass The Bluffs Lodge and park at the lot below the water tower. Read the placard to learn about the Caudill family, then walk to the overlook above the mountain cove. Can you believe what you just learned?

Return to the parkway and make a mental note to arrive here sometime to have the buckwheat pancakes in The Bluffs Restaurant, one of the older restaurants on this roadway. This old-fashioned breakfast will start a morning right.

Continue south on the parkway, through the Alligator Back turns, past a small family cemetery, out of Doughton Park and past Laurel Springs, one of the coldest spots in the state. This is the intersection of State 18, which leads south to Wilkesboro or west and north to loop back to Sparta on US 21, a lovely valley ride through the old community of Whitehead.

Butterflies perch on wildflowers on their way south

New River Christmas Tree Country

South of Laurel Springs on the parkway at milepost 258 you'll arrive at the turnoff to Glendale Springs, marked by the Northwest Trading Post. This parkway concession (open from mid-April through mid-November) is an outlet for local and regional crafts, dry goods, nonperishable foods, and baked goods.

After a browse here, drive into the heart of this small rural community, dominated by a grand Victorian house that once was the Glendale Springs Inn and Restaurant. Go past Lee's Motel and Restaurant (open for all meals from April through November). At the stop sign, State 16, continue straight; at the next stop sign turn right.

Glendale Springs is the site of Holy Trinity Episcopal Church, which is 100 yards from any obvious parking place you'll find. Artist Ben Long painted the remarkable fresco "The Last Supper" in the church, transforming a simple country place of worship into a much-visited shrine. The unassuming pews and interior of the sanctuary offset Long's magnificent painting in plaster, which is the backdrop for the altar. The church is open daily; a prerecorded message narrates the story of the fresco. Downstairs, in the undercroft, is another fresco, "Departure of Christ," by Jeffrey Mims, commissioned by a member of the congregation as a memorial to a ten year old. This tour also includes the frescoes in St. Mary's Church in West Jefferson.

Across the street is The Greenhouse Crafts Shop, where owners Joan and Michael Bell display an eclectic assemblage of crafts and seasonal decorations. Spontaneous performances of hammered dulcimer music are a common occurrence as Michael Bell steps behind the counter to serenade customers with his masterful playing of traditional mountain music.

The Mountain Bakery and Restaurant next door offers ample sandwiches and sweet samplers such as lemon and blueberry cream cheese squares, brownies, and fresh-baked breads. Across the street from the bakery is Silver Designs by Lou, the studio where artist Lou Eremita works in sterling silver. The School House Gallery displays the work of other area artists.

Return to State 16, the road in front of the Glendale Springs Inn, and turn right (south). In two miles, State 163 departs northwest from State 16, a right turn, leading eight miles deeper into the heart of Ashe County, and the communities of West Jefferson and Jefferson, the county seat.

The route crosses the south fork of the New River and then runs along Beaver Creek. On the way you'll pass the entrance to Mount Jefferson State Park, which is the obvious mountain on the east side of the highway. There is some geological mystery as to why Mount Jefferson is an isolated mountain, but mystery aside, this state park, crowned by a firetower, offers commanding vistas of the surrounding countryside. The summit is 4,684 feet above sea level, with overlooks that are breathtaking in more ways than one.

State 163 eventually arrives at a point of decision at the US 221 bypass, which, if taken, will speed you around the southeastern outskirts of the two communities and send you on the return ride. We opt here for the lengthier ride, of course.

Ashe County is pushing the borders of North Carolina west to Tennessee and north to Virginia. Locally, it has been considered one of the "Lost Provinces" (along with Alleghany County), the lay of the land encouraging more trade with neighboring states than with neighboring counties in its own state. As you certainly realize by now, once you are on top of the mountain, it is easier to stay up there. Some of the loveliest farmland you will ever see is within the borders of Ashe County.

Historically, Ashe County was claimed for a time by France, then belonged to the independent state of Franklin, then spent some time as part of Surry and Wilkes County before settling in as a county in 1799.

Thomas Jefferson was president in 1803 when the boundaries were drawn for the county seat, which was named for him. West Jefferson, the slightly smaller, more commercial neighbor, incorporated officially in 1915.

As mentioned, West Jefferson has a frescoed church, St. Mary's Episcopal Church. In this charming Carpenter Gothic Chapel, artist Ben Long painted the frescoes "Mary, Great with Child," "St. John the Baptist," and "The Mystery of Faith." The church is on Beaver Creek Road. To reach it from State 163, cross the US 221/State 88 bypass as though heading directly into West Jefferson on State 194/US 221. Turn left, onto Beaver Creek Road at McDonald's Restaurant. A small wooden sign notes the turn. Although St. Mary's is perhaps lesser known than Holy Trinity, because of its creekside-bend-in-the-road setting, it is a more picturesque church, with equally moving artwork inside.

Reverse your route back to State 194/US 221 business to enter West Jefferson. Downtown is a wonderfully compact and clearly defined business area, a working mountain downtown. In December, in conjunction with the annual choose and cut Christmas Tree Weekend, West Jefferson hosts an annual Studio Hop, a countywide open house to the arts. The Ashe County Arts Council sponsors the event, which routes you studio to studio around the mountain roads to see the work of local artisans on their home turf.

Follow US 221 business to Jefferson. This was the town where noted Harvard botanist Asa Gray lived while studying the flora of the region in 1841.

From here there are two ways to reach Sparta: via US 221, or via State 88 to Laurel Springs and then State 18 to Sparta. Most residents prefer the latter route even though it's longer, because US 221 is a meandering highway. Local humor says that the quickest way to get the governor to assist with roads here is to ride him in the back of an ambulance on US 221 from Jefferson to Sparta.

State 88 crosses the South Fork of the New River at the community of Index. At the crossing, State 16 turns south. If you're in the mood to do some canoeing, follow State 16 for half a mile to Zaloo's Canoes, one of the canoe rental groups for the New River. The New is an easy, if not outright lazy, canoeing river, with few rapids that are threatening, a few that will rock the boat, and one, from personal experience, that will tip your canoe and Tyler, too. Zaloo's offers a range of trips in miles, hours, and days, using the portage available at nearby Wagoner Access of the New River State Park as well as several takeouts long used by canoeists. Wagoner Access and the New River State Park headquarters are accessible off SR 1590, a left turn that is a little less than one and a half miles from the State 16/88 New River bridge.

The New River's designation as a National Wild and Scenic River is a long, complicated story that is legendary in the headwaters country. The river defines the countryside with its meandering, fresh clear water that harbors small-mouth bass and muskellunge. The river is far older than the mountains through which it flows, though geologists are unsure exactly how old it is. One indicator of its age is its shallow depth; nearly everywhere along it, you can almost walk across. Be that as it may, wear a life preserver if you go canoeing.

In the midseventies, the Appalachian Power Company proposed building a dam to create a pump storage facility on the New River. The proposed location was just south and west of Galax, Virginia, and would have created two tremen-

New River Christmas Tree Country

dous impoundments for electrical generation during peak demand only.

The fight to save the river went from the farmsteads of western North Carolina to the halls of Congress, resulting in the designation of 26.5 miles of the river as wild and scenic. As a part of those conditions, North Carolina established the New River State Park, creating several access areas along the river.

Return to State 88 and continue south past one of the loveliest farms you'll see—a North Carolina State University agricultural experimental farm.

State 88 joins State 18 at Laurel Springs in Alleghany County. Before turning left to go to Sparta, turn right to see the sights of the Laurel Springs Cafe and General Store, the very unusual, eclectic collection of Linda Woodie. Then rejoin State 18 to Sparta, or join the Blue Ridge Parkway north to return to US 21.

State 18 delivers you into Sparta at the town's principal traffic light on Main Street, which is also the intersection with US 21, and is the courthouse square of this small, rarely busy county seat. Find a place to park and enjoy the short walk through the central business area. You might want to sample a hot lunch at the town's oldest eatery, the Sparta Restaurant, across from the courthouse.

Another interesting diversion is Farmer's Hardware on the corner of State 18 and Main Street. The old-time helpfulness and hospitality are a throwback to another era.

If you're interested in local crafts or delicious baked goods, turn left (west) at the light and travel about half a mile on US 21 to Country Homestead Antiques, on the left in an old house, just past the Sparta School. This enterprise features mountain crafts and delicious home-baked brownies, chess squares, and cream cheese confections. The collectibles vary slightly with the season; the real discovery is the bakery.

If you continue out of town on US 21, you will come to the junction with US 221 (from Jefferson, remember?). Turn right onto US 221 north and continue about five miles from the intersection, just before crossing the New River. On your right is New River Canoe & Campground, Inc., one of the oldest outfitters on the river. Dwayne Murphy operates this business, which offers tubing, pedal boats, and canoes and any number of trips, complete with portage.

One of Sparta's biggest weekends (besides its wonderful Fourth of July parade) is Choose and Cut Weekend, the oldest Christmas tree selection weekend in the area, held the first weekend of December. The Sparta Chamber of Commerce hosts a tent display with hot cider at the corner of Main Street and Valley View Drive, showing the different species of trees and the location of the various farms.

Follow US 21 south out of Sparta, across the Little River, renowned among canoeists for its six-foot drop. On this road, across from the old Dr. Graybow pipe factory, is Hawks Produce, the seasonal produce stand of the family by that name. You'll find delicious honey of several mountain trees (among them sourwood and locust) and several old-time apple varieties, such as Magnum Bonum, a red apple that's tart enough to cook with, sweet enough to eat. Hawks carries pumpkins as big as Buicks for Halloween and ornamental gourds and corn for the Thanksgiving table. The shop is a grand resource with much country atmosphere.

Follow US 21 south back to the Blue Ridge Parkway and on to Roaring Gap. If you're hungry, before you reach the parkway, turn north on SR 1444 in Glade Valley to go to Marion's Old Homeplace, a half mile away. Marion's serves family-style country cooking and stays busy and full. You will be too. Full and satisfied is the way you ought to feel after this tour. It's a good way to go home.

New River Christmas Tree Country

In the Area

Stone Mountain State Park (Traphill): 910-957-8185

Blue Ridge Parkway, Bluffs Ranger District: 910-372-8568 or 910-372-8867

Pine Shadows Farm (Roaring Gap): 910-363-2890

Mountain Hearth Lodge & Restaurant, 910-372-8743

The Bluffs Lodge (Doughton Park): 910-372-4499

Northwest Trading Post (Glendale Springs): 910-982-2543

The Greenhouse Crafts Shop (Glendale Springs): 910-982-2618

Mount Jefferson State Park (West Jefferson): 910-246-9643

Zaloo's Canoes (Index): 910-246-3066

New River State Park (Wagoner): 910-982-2587

Laurel Springs Cafe & General Store (Laurel Springs): 910-359-2564

Country Homestead Antiques (Sparta): 910-372-8851

New River Canoe & Campground, Inc. (Sparta): 910-372-8793

Marion's Old Homeplace (Glade Valley): 910-372-4676

New River Country Travel Association (accommodations or recreational information): 919-982-9414

Alleghany County Chamber of Commerce (Sparta): 910-372-5473

Ashe County Chamber of Commerce (West Jefferson): 910-246-9550

4 ~ A Cool Glide at the End of the Ride

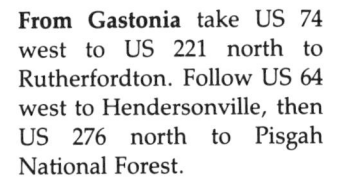

From Gastonia take US 74 west to US 221 north to Rutherfordton. Follow US 64 west to Hendersonville, then US 276 north to Pisgah National Forest.

Highlights: *Crowders Mountain State Park; Shelby and its historic district; Rutherfordton's cottage architecture; Lake Lure; Chimney Rock Park; and Pisgah National Forest and Sliding Rock.*

Imagine that you are writhing in one of those nearly insufferable summer days that drive you to drink. This tour does just that—sort of—routing you across the ridge-top roads, river valley bottomlands, and majestic gorges to deliver you at one of nature's surefire cures for the heat, Sliding Rock Recreation Area in the Pisgah National Forest. The drive takes about three hours one way if you don't stop. The problem is, there's more than enough to do in one day or three. I just love the drive.

This tour begins southwest of Gastonia on I-85. Take exit 13 off the interstate, then turn south, crossing over I-85 to the junction of US 74.

A Cool Glide at the End of the Ride

Head west a short way on US 74 until you see the signs indicating Crowders Mountain State Park. Turn left on Sparrow Spring Road. From this point it's a few miles to the park office, but the routing is kind of tricky. Avoid the turn labeled Crowders Mountain Country Club, and follow the road as it veers right. Sparrow Spring Road continues to a stop sign at an island in the road; turn right to reach the front gates of the park.

The Crowders Mountain Trail begins near the park headquarters and ascends to the top of the mountain after crossing back over Sparrow Spring Road. The trail will give you a good workout, rewarding the time and exertion with a rich natural passage and a spectacular view.

The route takes you through some impressive geological formations. The peaks of the King's Pinnacle and Crowders Mountain are part of a rock formation known to geologists as the Kings Mountain Belt. This geological feature began long ago as sedimentary deposits, then metamorphosed into quartzite, a very hard, erosion-resistant rock. Great forces in the earth turned it on edge, and erosion has completed the sculpting.

The results are spectacular: 100- to 150-foot cliffs on Crowders Mountain, ideal for rock climbing. Crowders Mountain rises 750 feet above the surrounding terrain, and 1,625 feet above sea level. The King's Pinnacle is 80 feet taller. If you catch a clear day, it offers a marvelous vista of the Charlotte skyline, whether or not you're tethered to a climbing rope.

The north side of the mountain, which has been spared from heavy timbering, is a repository of vegetation, such as rhododendron, that is more typical of higher elevations elsewhere in the state. In the early part of the twentieth century, an "All Healing Springs" seeped from the northeast side of the mountain, which resulted in the construction of a hotel for invalid guests so that they might "take the waters."

Two decades ago, a statewide concern was that people were planning to take the rocks as well. Crowders Mountain is rich in kyanite, aluminum, and lithium. Subsequent to their discovery, their mineral wealth began to be realized. The movement to save Crowders Mountain originated from a need to protect it from wholesale destruction since, at the time, the state had few prohibitions against surface mining.

Local citizens urged preservation of the landmarks, and the state purchased Crowders Mountain in the early 1970s, adding King's Pinnacle more than a decade later. That is why there is a state park here.

After making the hike to Crowders Mountain or to the King's Pinnacle, return to US 74 the way you entered. Turn west on US 74 and take the US 74 bypass around Kings Mountain.

Pull over, stop the car, lower the top, put on your shades, and raise your expectations. This is a road for ragtop cruising.

The farther you travel through the rolling countryside, the more you feel as though Cleveland County may have been kept a secret from the rest of the state for several reasons. First, the wind from the ridge-top roads scrubs the countryside clean; beyond the roadside bungalows, the vistas open to farms and wooded creeks.

There is, for me, the echo of another place and time. Were there no trees, this would be grassland. In fact, much of the land along this route was prairie in the early eighteenth century. The Colonial settlers who moved into this region in the 1700s found American bison and elk roaming the grassland and foraging through the intermittent woods. More likely than not, lightning set fires that kept forested growth at bay. The animals would move freely on the grasslands and graze on the high ridges above the streams and creeks. It was along these watercourses that the Catawba Nation of Native Americans thrived, constructing sheltered villages to create communities sustained by agriculture and trade.

A Cool Glide at the End of the Ride

The plains are gone, of course, and so are the animals, but still there is a distinctive character to US 74. A planting of white pines and sycamore trees lines the roadway six miles east of Shelby—man's hand shaping the landscape. Testimony to a bygone chapter of natural history is found in two miles—the crossing of Buffalo Creek, one of many such creeks in the state with that name.

Look to either side of the road and you can imagine the buffalo roaming the plains, dropping down into the creeks to drink. The roadway feels as though it is perched above the surrounding area, imparting a breezy feeling to the passage.

As you approach Shelby on US 74, drive past the exit for US 74 business and continue on the bypass. Now I realize that this is a hurried, focused trip, but still, you must see Shelby. Turn right on South Washington Street and follow it to the center of town. South Washington is part of the Central Shelby Historic District, which is listed on the National Register of Historic Places. I suspect what you find will surprise you. Shelby's central business area is one of the most attractive community centers in the state, just as "uptown" as their merchant support group touts it to be.

It's evident that the district is not homogeneous, but there are some fine places indeed next to public rights-of-way. The town more than merits a walking tour. A brochure is available at the Cleveland County Chamber of Commerce, at 200 South Lafayette Street. (Lafayette Street parallels South Washington Street one block to the west.)

In 1907, county leaders built the courthouse where it could be seen, smack in the middle of a square, surrounded as it is with tree-lined streets and small shops. The lovely streets are a tribute to the efforts of the North Carolina Main Street Program, designed to provide small towns with assistance in maintaining appearance and viability downtown.

The old courthouse makes a logical starting point for a walking tour because it is central, and is now the home of the Cleveland County Historical Society. The walking tour fans out from the commercial center and takes about two hours to do completely.

Walk one block east to South Washington and continue to 403 South Washington, the house known as Webbley. This mid-eighteenth-century residence was the home of Judge James L. Webb, whose daughter Fay married O. Max Gardner, governor of the state (from 1929 to 1933) and initiator of what would be known as the Shelby Dynasty of statewide political power. The run of excellent political fortune continued through the early 1950s, ending with the death of U.S. Senator Clyde R. Hoey in 1954. The vestiges of the power in this community are the homes that are in the historic district or just outside it.

Webbley is now a bed and breakfast, meticulously restored to the grandeur of its time. There are expressions of other dreams in Shelby, such as the Gibbs House at 520 West Warren Street. Also known as "El Nido," the Nest, this is a fanciful California bungalow constructed to satisfy the homesickness of a dentist's wife far from her native state. Strongly influenced by Spanish heritage, El Nido is one of the rarest architectural treasures in the state.

Shelby strikes me as a community whose day in the state limelight endured as a shining beacon but then faded, although the physical expressions of that success—the buildings and the commercial core—never vanished. The downtown refuses to relinquish its proper place as a community center and, through the innovative efforts of the Main Street Program, and the determination of its citizens, bustles into a new era that is building on its politically regal past with an egalitarian spirit.

Politics were not everything, though powerful voices who captured the passion of regional politics also rest here,

A Cool Glide at the End of the Ride

such as W. J. Cash, who wrote *The Mind of the South*, an influential book on the attitudes of the South. Thomas Dixon, Jr., author of *The Clansman*, later made into the movie *The Birth of a Nation*, also rests here. Dixon, strangely, was an ardent conservationist and was very influential, with other sportsmen residents of northeast North Carolina, in the founding of Ducks Unlimited.

Return to the US 74 bypass to begin a beautiful, long uphill climb. This is where the road seems to lay the land to either side open like a book. There are several signs indicating turns south to Boiling Springs, a small community named for springs known to the Cherokee Indians. The community was incorporated in 1909 and is perhaps better known as the site of Gardner-Webb University and its 200-acre campus.

Is the top down yet? What do you want in a highway if it isn't this passage through Cleveland County, a lovely rolling passage that is no doubt highway but every bit a country road? There's a little bit of civilization, just not too much, and there's none of the hermetic sterility that comes with an interstate, nor is it as jaded as an old thoroughfare that "progress" has transformed into an industrial/commercial wasteland. It simply imparts a real sweet feeling in the car, not isolated but not crowded either, just country.

Continue past Mooresboro and the signs indicating the upcoming communities of Forest City and Spindale, the latter named for a cotton mill established there in the late nineteenth century.

On the left will be the buildings for Isothermal Community College, perhaps the most unusually named community college in the statewide system. Parts of Rutherford County and neighboring Polk County are in a thermal belt. In its simplest explanation, it means that the temperatures at the base of the mountains tend to be disproportionately warmer than the air higher up, far warmer in fact than typical temperature variation based on changes in elevation. Accordingly, there are few frosts and killing freezes.

This peculiarity, noted in the nineteenth century, ameliorates the effects of sudden warming, followed by sudden freezing; in short, there is a very brief frost season and a lengthy growing season. This cycle in these latitudes lays aside the terror that sudden freezes strike in the hearts of orchard owners awaiting successful pollination and fruit set. In thermal belt plantations, the threat is nearly eliminated altogether. Something else it does too, it makes the region simply delicious as far as taking the sting out of summer. You'll see more on that in a bit.

Exit US 74 to join US 221 north, the road to Rutherfordton. You'll pass an orchard, one of many in this part of southern Rutherford County. From the end of August through early September, workers will still be picking peaches.

After a zoo of Kudzu critters on the south side of the highway, US 221 brings you into the heart of this mountain town, which with neighboring Spindale and Forest City forms a "tri-city" commercial hub in the area. US 221 intersects US 74 business on the fringe of Rutherfordton's downtown. Turn left on US 74 and follow it as it bends around a structure that must have been the major manufacturer in the community. On the right will be the Old Rutherfordton City Hall–Fire Department building.

Historic markers fix the frontier outpost and crossroads nature of the community in history: the Overmountain men passed this way en route to Kings Mountain in 1780, an ambitious immigrant operated a mint here until 1849, and the ubiquitous Stoneman brought his cavalry troop through here during the Civil War.

The road turns into a visual treat of bungalows. The turn-of-the-century cottage architecture reveals seasonal influxes

A Cool Glide at the End of the Ride

of those who would escape the heat of lower elevations. The homes look like mountain getaways; many of them are the subject of head-turning restorations—nothing ornate, just faithful and inherently honest to their era. I reluctantly departed Rutherfordton, as charming a small town as it's been my pleasure to pass through in a long time, imparting a solid feeling of community.

Just outside of town, US 64 merges with US 74. This is the route to continue west the twenty miles to Lake Lure and on to Chimney Rock. Quickly, however, you get the feeling that these will not be speedy miles. Sure enough, US 64/74 waggles toward Lake Lure like a dog shaking its tail. It's an easy drive, but you will be turning the wheel a lot. Got the top down yet?

Shortly after passing the Nothing Fancy Cafe, and an unusual roadside reminder reference to the Book of John 3:16, you pass what I call a Georgia mountain, which is simply a small mountain timbered and replanted in loblolly pine. That's fine for Georgia, where the loblolly is king of the reforested mountain, but typically in these latitudes and on such terrain, white pine is the tree of choice. This hill, unremarkable otherwise, gives me a visual nudge to the south. In ten more years, somebody will turn these trees into a downpayment on a house or a college education.

As you come into Whitesides, also known as Pumpkin Center, take note in particular of one farmhouse backing up against the Rocky Broad River. This is where the Whiteside family has grown pumpkins from the same homestead since the early 1800s. The old variety they cultivate—turning yellow, not bright orange—makes for good eating.

The log structure on your left is a reconstruction of old Russel's Fort, named after George Russel, who was killed by Indians on a bear hunt after the Revolutionary War.

There is only a hint that you are moving into a mountain setting, and this is what makes Lake Lure so enticing. US 64/74 crosses the river on an old concrete bridge; adjacent to it, there's an old country store that has been remodeled into the headquarters of a small construction company.

A welcome sign alerts you to the hospitality of the Hickory Nut Gorge Chamber of Commerce, noting also that Lake Lure was incorporated in 1927. Suddenly you see the Point of View restaurant, and walls of rock. The effect is stunning.

Lake Lure looks delightfully like a 1920s summer place, when America was indeed simpler and perhaps gentler. The route continues around the west side of the lake, past a volunteer fire department and a golf course with a log cabin as the clubhouse.

Continue past the junction of State 9 on the left. After the modest Lake Lure Post Office, the road swirls around the stylish Lake Lure Inn. Behind it seems to be the world's biggest rock wall, which forms the south buttress of Hickory Nut Gorge, from which protrudes Chimney Rock. It's an "oh, my" vista—the white-sand beach, the venerable roaring twenties Lake Lure Inn, and a boardwalk between the road and the lake, which leads to the municipal marina.

The Rocky Broad River took a few hundred million years to whittle this canyon named Hickory Nut Gorge, one of the most scenic valleys in North Carolina. Agreed? In fact, Hollywood filmed portions of *Dirty Dancing* and *The Last of the Mohicans* here. Anybody with celluloid can do well; there is no end to the spectacular scenery—and fall color comes late and hangs around awhile. The view is also stunning from the lake. Pontoon boat tours of the 1,500-acre lake and its twenty-eight miles of shoreline are available in the town of Lake Lure.

This lake exists because of the promotional wizardry of Dr. Lucius B. Morse, a man who found this region by chance because he had tuberculosis. Morse came to nearby Hendersonville because of the mild climate and soon discovered

A Cool Glide at the End of the Ride

Chimney Rock (just beyond Lake Lure), which had been open to tourists since 1885. Morse enlisted the aid of his brothers and bought the promontory in 1902. From then on, Chimney Rock grew in size and attractiveness as a destination as Morse made continual improvements. The biggest came in 1927 when the Morse brothers constructed a 115-foot-high, 600-foot-long dam across the Rocky Broad River, flooding the cruciform-shaped valley and creating Lake Lure. The inn was constructed, and building lots were steadily sold. Because of the area's unsurpassed physical beauty and its proximity to population centers, it became a social center of international renown.

The entrance to Chimney Rock Park is evident just beyond Lake Lure. Here you can ascend to some breathtaking views of the man-made lake and the gorge itself. A winding three-mile drive brings you to a parking lot where you can hike or ride an elevator nearly to the top of Chimney Rock. Come prepared for a breathless hike of chutes and ladders; a network of boardwalks and trails provides access to the natural highlights of the nearly 1,000-acre preserve.

Of the multiple trails to choose from, one is a must—the Skyline Trail from Chimney Rock to the top of 404-foot Hickory Nut Falls. This is a challenging walk; bring a canteen and take your time: you'll be ready with a sigh for the sign at Exclamation Point that reads, "The toughest part of the trail is behind you." The hike is worth it: the best view is right beside the sign. The trip back catwalks alongside sheer cliffs.

Seeing the remainder of the park—thoroughly exploring Moonshiner's Cave, threading the Eye-of-the-Needle, or walking to the base of Hickory Nut Falls—can take the better part of a day. It's one of the best six or seven dollars you'll spend.

Take time to poke around the town of Chimney Rock, a weathered mountain retreat with a "cottagey" feel. You'll find the cozy Dogwood Inn between US 64/74 and the river, and its neighbor the Gingerbread Inn, looking just as inviting.

Chimney Rock

A Cool Glide at the End of the Ride

For some old-time hospitality, step inside Bubba's General Store and say hello to Bubba (he's the dog). Peek at the waterfall out back and enjoy the easygoing nature of this little spot. Follow the gorge upstream on US 64/74, past Hickory Nut Falls Campground, to see the wonderfully sited Evening Shade River Lodging. These are charming little sheds hanging out over the edge of the river; no two floors are the same level, nor are any two roofs. The buildings just march right alongside the river.

Just before Bat Cave the highway swings around the elegant 1890 Esmeralda Inn, the oldest hostelry in the gorge. Let the shade of the live oaks roll right over you; the front porch begs you to rock awhile.

Bat Cave is named for the obvious: the cave harbors these endangered mammals. There are several little roadside stores and one elegant multigabled residence, converted to a boutique known as "A Touch in Time."

In the town of Bat Cave, turn west on US 64, crossing the river and continuing to Hendersonville. For the first six miles, US 64 follows Reedy Patch Creek, ascending to the headwaters—a lovely waterside drive. Once the road emerges from the gorge, in the small community of Edneyville, it rides the plateau, passing through rolling countryside.

It's time to steel yourself for the tedious passage through Hendersonville, the seat of Henderson County, which dates from 1838. Since the mid-1970s, Hendersonville has grown steadily as a retirement community; its paired thoroughfares move you as quickly as possible through town. The fact is, Hendersonville is squeezed a mite by growth. If you are a literary buff or a pursuer of things nostalgic, keep an eye out for the cemetery off US 64 at West Sixth Avenue. The headstone for Margaret E. Johnson became the inspiration for the title of Asheville author Thomas Wolfe's literary signature, *Look Homeward, Angel.*

Should you detour slightly south of Hendersonville on US 25 (now you realize why it takes me so long to go anywhere), you will arrive in Flat Rock, the aristocrat of North Carolina's mountaintop vacation communities. It is the home of the Flat Rock Playhouse, the Carl Sandburg Home and National Historic Site—Connemara—which is open to the public, and also to the elegant pre–Civil War Woodfield Inn. Flat Rock, named for a Cherokee assembly, is the original early-nineteenth-century mountain retreat for wealthy Charlestonians; as a community it has significant historic value and visual appeal. In truth, much of what you would like to see stands sequestered behind vegetation. It is a quiet and private place.

One of the more treasured buildings in the area is St. John in the Wilderness, an Episcopal summer chapel designed by Charleston architect E. C. Jones in 1852 on a site already hallowed by family burials. It is a serene chapel with a corner tower and buttressed walls with Low Country–style shutters, echoing the origin of the Flat Rock community. Jones also designed The Flat Rock Hotel, known today as the Woodfield Inn, embellishing that structure with stylish lattice ornamentation. There's enough poking around in Flat Rock to consume another of those days that this intended-to-be-direct itinerary warns of in the beginning.

I will suppose that you went to Flat Rock anyway, so return to Hendersonville, again take up US 64 west, and this time don't stop. The drive is a helter-skelter winding road, curling around Jumpoff Mountain and Horseshoe Mountain, dancing beside the headwaters of the French Broad River, and rambling past a scramble of new retirement communities, commercial ventures, and older settled farms. The mountains to the north are part of the massive Pisgah Ridge, much of

A Cool Glide at the End of the Ride

their acreage in Pisgah National Forest. The road closely follows a railroad track that goes from Hendersonville to Brevard. At the very least it is one remarkable valley passage.

Turn right (north) on US 276 and enter Pisgah National Forest, stopping at the intersection for an ice cream cone from one of several vendors (in season, of course). The Pisgah Ranger Station is on the right just as you pass Sycamore Flats picnic area. The Davidson River Campground is on your left.

The Pisgah Ranger District includes 157,000 acres, some of which is wilderness, ranging in elevation from 2,000 feet to more than 6,100 feet. There are 250 miles of hiking trails, and visitor centers at the Pisgah Forest National Fish Hatchery, six miles above the Pisgah Ranger Station, and at the Cradle of Forestry in America. At the Cradle of Forestry, interpretive exhibits reconstruct the first days of forestry practice in the United States under the leadership of Gifford Pinchot and Dr. Carl Schenck.

As you drive north along the Davidson River on US 276, you will probably see cars parked along the highway and travelers gawking at the sixty-foot cascade of Looking Glass Falls. The river widens approximately twelve miles north of the ranger station. The traffic slows, and you'll see a very large parking area with a bathhouse. You'll hear squeals of laughter as you drive in. This is Sliding Rock, the reason you drove three hours in the summer heat.

Even in August's most brutal broil, the Davidson River hisses over Sliding Rock at an invigorating fifty-three to fifty-eight degrees Fahrenheit. There are two types of visitors to this very popular water feature: them that slides, and them that don't and says they did.

Here's what happens: You edge out into the river, up at the top of the rock. You sit down into the spine-liquefying chill that swirls up around your dimpling derriere. Then you inch forward, slowly, under the illusion that you are controlling your fate. Slowly forward, until you can't stop. Gravity and the river own your arrogant mass, and the two are discharging you due south into . . . the coldest water on earth.

Your chest constricts, your eyes bulge, something inside your body yells a heavenly supplication. The river spits you out like the shaved, disheveled, ice water–subdued convert that you are. It makes you righteous; it makes you go again.

After all, that's why you took this quickie tour anyway.

In the Area

Crowders Mountain State Park (Gastonia): 704-853-5375

Cleveland County Chamber of Commerce (Shelby): 704-487-8521

Cleveland County Historical Society (Shelby): 704-481-1842

The Inn at Webbley (Shelby): 704-481-1043

Whiteside Pumpkin Center (Whitesides): 704-286-9438

Chimney Rock Park (Chimney Rock): 800-277-9611

Hickory Nut Gorge Chamber of Commerce (Chimney Rock): 704-625-2725

Bubba's General Store (Chimney Rock): 704-625-2479

Esmeralda Inn (Chimney Rock): 704-625-9105

A Touch in Time (Bat Cave): 704-625-1902

Pisgah National Forest Ranger Station, 704-877-3265

5 ~ Old Greensboro–Chapel Hill Road and Some Extras

From Greensboro: Take US 421 south to the Alamance Church Road, then County 1005, the Greensboro–Chapel Hill Road, then unnumbered but named back roads to Chapel Hill and beyond.

Highlights: Old mill sites, graveyards, and churches; picturesque farmhouses and barns; Niche Gardens; Carrboro and Chapel Hill; Jordan Lake with houseboat rentals and a glimpse of bald eagles; Fearrington and its belted galloways; Bynum's chain saw–sculpted "critters."

This easy-on-the-eyes tour is through the long-settled but remarkably uncrowded Piedmont. The route, which follows a diagonal path southeast, becomes a succession of ridge-top and creek-bottom crossings.

A few miles outside of Greensboro on Alamance Church Road, you'll pass an old farmhouse behind a chain-link fence. Shortly after that is a long red cedar–lined driveway marked by a sign for Neese's Country Sausage, at 1452 Alamance Church Road. This certainly was country when they opened their doors; in 1993 this local institution celebrated its seventy-fifth anniversary of putting large pigs into one-pound packages, using "everything but the squeal."

The plant is wholesale only, but it does allow church groups and civic organizations to purchase directly. It's a business that definitely retains an old-time, family-owned flavor.

Road names stencil the history and the early citizens of the region at eye height—fodder for the imagination. You'll pass Wiley Davis Road, Nelson Farm Road, and Williams Dairy Road—a clue to land use and important features of the early agricultural landscape. Shortly after the intersection of Nelson Farm Road, you'll see a steeple framed by the roadside trees and a fork in the road. The main route goes right, but take the left fork, Presbyterian Road, which loops around the graveyard and grounds of the Alamance Presbyterian Church, founded in 1764 by the Scotch-Irish settlers who convened on these frontier lands. The church deed describes the corners of the property by reference to landmarks, such as a spring, that are no longer evident.

Mill Point Road intersects Presbyterian Road near the church. The "Mill Point" is three miles away at a beautiful crossing of Little Alamance Creek. The remains of buildings are powerful evidence of the importance of waterpower to early settlers.

Once again road names are descriptive—Young's Mill Road and Brookhaven Mill Road terminate at Mill Point Road. Each road will lead you to an old mill site along Little Alamance Creek.

Double back to Alamance Presbyterian Church; turn left on Presbyterian Road and left again on Alamance Church Road.

You're "in-country" now, leaving behind Greensboro's population spillover. The road passes an auto salvage yard, negotiates S curves, crosses the bottomland of the two forks of Big Alamance Creek, and winds around Walnut Woods Golf

Old Greensboro–Chapel Hill Road and Some Extras

Course at the intersection of Scythe and Alamance Church Roads. There's a log cabin on the left.

About 1.5 miles past the golf course, at the intersection of Old Julian Road, is C&H Gas and Groceries. The letters stand for Clarence and Hattie, the owners. This is definitely an independently owned and operated country store.

Continue straight to the next intersection, State 62, the new Julian Road. A Texaco station marks it. Continue straight, past the E-Z Ride Ass and Mule Farm, which raises mules and asses. North Carolina's Bicycle Highway Route 2 joins your road at this intersection, a testimony to the scenic quality and manageable traffic on the route.

You'll cross Stinking Quarter Creek and pass the Mt. Pleasant United Methodist Church on the south side of the road before coming face to face with Kimesville Lake.

Actually, you'll see the remarkable rock dam of Kimesville Lake, which was built in 1812. This very small community honors the Kime, or perhaps Keim family, German immigrants who settled here in the mid–eighteenth century. By 1788, the first mill began operating; what remains is the rock dam.

Just after the Alamance County sign, you'll turn right onto SR 1005, the Greensboro–Chapel Hill Road. This is the time for a run in the country, past a few small residences hugging the old route. The edges of the woods advance and recede from the pavement in a pattern of cultivation and preservation.

An exquisite farmhouse, larger than any previously passed, on the north side of the road signals the approach of State 49, the route between Burlington (to the north) and Liberty. The Elliott Grocery Store commands the intersection. A sign indicates you have twenty-seven miles to go to Chapel Hill.

The countryside seems to relax, and in late October it beckons with that characteristic weedy, scruffy Piedmont appearance that is absent in the eastern part of the state, where the land is flatter and the plow furrows more cleanly from fence line to fence line. The cornstalks are down and the earth looks reddish and raw.

The intersection with Coble Mill Road calls to mind the tendency of families to stay close to the land, to be fruitful and multiply. The Cobles were so numerous that a township in Alamance County bore their name, as does this district's U.S. congressman, Howard Coble, and a dairy, and the mill road.

A small church and graveyard appear abruptly on the north side of the road, which climbs beside them, then dips to an intersection. Stop. Turn left past the Cane Creek Meeting (the road sign indicates Chapel Hill). The building is the site of the first (1751) monthly meeting of the Society of Friends, also known as the Quakers, who settled much of the central Piedmont of North Carolina. The present church is on the original site of the meeting.

Very shortly you will be in Snow Camp, so named because after the March 15, 1781, battle of Guilford Courthouse, in the present city limits of Greensboro, the British troops under the command of Lord Charles Cornwallis camped here in the snow. The town is an old Quaker community; in summer, it is the site of the outdoor drama *The Sword of Peace*, the story of the pacifist Quakers in the years leading up to the Revolutionary War.

Continue east past Lindley Mill Road, which bears the name of an early family prominent in local history. On the right, directly beside the road, is the Spring Friends Meeting House, which dates from 1761. Note the Gothic windows.

In the community of Eli Whitney, at the intersection of State 87, I talked with the proprietor of Ray's Quick Stop, who wore a hat with the inscription, "Eli Whitney, the crossroads of the world."

Although many people have come and gone this way, Eli Whitney was not one of them. The town name came from a cotton gin that was here, but it seems that "the gin gave out," and the building became a school and the name stuck. The school gave out, too, followed by another one, but by then folks wouldn't let go of the name. So they moved the name (not the school) down to the intersection so it and any wanderers wouldn't feel lost.

The price of a cold drink in Ray's, right in the crossroads of the world, bought that explanation.

Continue straight, past the community center and the softball field. This is great country, where the barns look like barns and the sugar maples are perfect front-yard lollipop shapes and the name of every crossroads hints at its pragmatic history.

You cross the Haw River and enter Orange County. The remaining nine or so miles to US 15-501 bypass around Carrboro and Chapel Hill are a pure pleasure to drive.

Niche Gardens, at 1111 Dawson Road, is marked by a small hand-painted sign on the south side of the highway at the Dawson Road intersection. This nursery, nestled in the pine woods, specializes in southeastern wildflowers and rare plants. They sell by mail-order catalog, but there are some on-site sales and tours of the garden. It is best to call for an appointment.

The road crests a small hill and plunges to a stop sign at Jones Ferry Road, where you turn left and cross University Lake, one of the water sources for Carrboro and Chapel Hill. You will come to the intersection of State 54, the Carrboro bypass.

For an interesting detour, poke your head into Carrboro by continuing directly into town on Jones Ferry Road. You may want to stop and see the Carr Mill Mall, a converted textile mill that houses specialty shops and is the largest building in town, on your left. You can grab a quick sandwich in the Spring Garden Bar and Grill, in the flatiron building where Jones Ferry Road and Main Street converge. Park where you can; the students from the University of North Carolina, just east of where you are, have the town parking lot filled, to say the least.

Carrboro's Main Street becomes Franklin Street in Chapel Hill, a terrific college town. It is a tour in its own right and not to be fully dealt with here, but I can't resist a few suggestions.

Stop at the Downtown Welcome Center in Chapel Hill—it's in the McDade House (the yellow brick house next to the First Baptist Church on West Franklin Street at the intersection of Columbia Street)—to pick up a copy of "A Walk Down Franklin Street." The Mast General Store, at 458 West Franklin Street, and Four Eleven West, a restaurant at 411 West Franklin Street, are worth exploring.

Turn south on Columbia Street and continue across the overpass bridge and the bridge across Morgan Creek. You're now on US 15-501 south, and with a left at the stoplight onto Mount Carmel Church Road, you're back on the tour.

A friend describes Mount Carmel Church Road as one of the finest motorcycle rides around. It's fine in a car, too. The road varies, the tree line pinches, then recedes as you climb easy hills and roll through twisting creek bottoms. Highway planners didn't design this road; wagons and horses did.

Not surprisingly, you'll see the little green signs with the numeral 2, indicating that you're back on the bike road again, and it is sometimes filled with cyclers. Be cautious; there's not much room for fancy maneuvering.

Old Greensboro–Chapel Hill Road and Some Extras

You will see the Whippoorwill Road intersection, a British Petroleum sign, and the 1803 Mount Carmel Baptist Church on the left at the Chatham County line. Mount Carmel Church Road ends where the Farrington Road merges from the east.

To the west is the ridge of Edwards Mountain, one of the higher landforms in the county. Along its slopes is the exclusive golf development named Governor's Cup.

The crossroads community of Farrington is next. Drive on south and cross the north end of B. Everett Jordan Lake, which is actually the flooded bottomlands of New Hope Creek. Stop at either end of the bridge and look with binoculars at the flats to the east. Sometimes in the treetops you can see bald eagles. Jordan Lake's impoundment and its characteristically shallow water brought the bonus of these birds. Some portions of the lake are closed to protect the nesting populations.

If you're looking for an unusual outing, rent a sport boat or a houseboat from Crosswinds Marina, visible from Farrington Road.

Just after the marina is a stone wall and a handsome early restored home. You'll sneak up on it.

Farrington Road intersects US 64 in Wilsonville, named for Cecil Wilson, who had a store here on the south side of the highway, where a store is today. If you turn left, you're on your way to Cary (fifteen miles) and Raleigh (twenty miles). Don't do it. Turn right.

The causeway across B. Everett Jordan Lake is a four-lane divided highway with an expansive view of the reservoir. Then the highway narrows, and for nearly two miles you are treated to a botanical wonder: the wooded slope on the south side of the highway has native mountain laurel, very unusual in these parts.

You'll ascend to a junction known as Griffins Crossroads, with a small wood-sided store on your left. Turn right. Signs indicate the way to US 15-501 and Bynum.

After passing a dairy farm, this gentle shortcut winds to a dead end at US 15-501. Turn right, go approximately one mile, and turn right into the entrance of the village of Fearrington.

You are now in Chatham County, between Chapel Hill and Pittsboro, but the village center here will make you think you're in England. The village of Fearrington is a well-to-do residential community, home to belted galloways, a breed of Irish cattle that is black on the ends and white in the middle—"Oreo angus," if you please.

Leave some daylight in your schedule to study the English country gardens crafted by owner Jenny Fitch. Shop at the specialty stores such as Dovecote, a country gardener's shop; the Pringle Pottery; and McIntyre's, a wonderful bookshop.

Looking for a special weekend? Try an overnight in the luxurious Fearrington House Inn and Restaurant. You should make dinner reservations well in advance for the elegant fine dining in this 1927 homeplace of the Fearrington family.

When you leave the village, turn left (south) on US 15-501 toward Pittsboro. Then turn left onto the Bynum Road, approximately three miles south of Fearrington. This spur carries you through the nearly abandoned mill town named for the Bynum family, who constructed the nineteenth-century cotton mill. Keep an eye to the left for a field filled with whimsical wooden "critters," the chain saw–sculpted menagerie of Clyde Jones, Bynum's most well-known resident. The animals are for your enjoyment, not for sale.

The homes in Bynum reflect the typical stratification of southern cotton mill towns, mill owners and mill workers. Look left as you cross the Haw River to see the mill; look right to see the millrace that carried water from an upstream dam to the mill.

Dovecote, a country gardener's shop

At the stop sign, turn left to continue to Pittsboro, the seat of Chatham County and the site of one of the state's most noticeable courthouses. The town greets you with a row of delightful old homes lining the road. Then US 15-501 and US 64 meet at a traffic circle dominated—no, commanded—by the Chatham County Courthouse. You have arrived on Hillsboro Street. East Street (US 64 east) leads to B. Everett Jordan Lake and Raleigh; West Street leads to Siler City; and US 15-501 is known as the Sanford Road.

There are several buildings of note in Pittsboro: the Masonic Lodge on East Street is one of the oldest in the state, and St. Bartholomew's Episcopal Church, an elegant Carpenter-Gothic chapel on Salisbury Street, perches amid the graves of parishioners.

Continue west on US 64 to the intersection of State 87 at the edge of town. Turn north; in sixteen miles of rural passage, you'll arrive at Eli Whitney—"crossroads of the world"—and that's arrivin'.

In the Area

Chapel Hill–Orange County Visitors Bureau (Chapel Hill): 919-968-2060

Alamance Presbyterian Church (Greensboro): 910-697-0488

Niche Gardens (near Carrboro): 919-967-0078

Four Eleven West (Chapel Hill): 919-967-2782

Crosswinds Marina (B. Everett Jordan Lake): 919-362-1615

Fearrington House Inn and Restaurant (Fearrington): 919-542-2121

6 ~ The Long-Needle Loop:

Sight-seeing in the Sandhills

From Charlotte: Take US 74 east to Rockingham and turn north on US 220. Drive to Ellerbe, nine miles north of Rockingham on US 220. **From Greensboro**, take US 220 south through Asheboro to the junction with State 211. Exit on 211 east to the traffic circle in Pinehurst. **From Raleigh,** follow US 1 south to Southern Pines. Exit on State 2 (Midland Road) to the traffic circle at Pinehurst.

Highlights: *The Rankin Museum of American Heritage in Ellerbe; Sandhills Agricultural Research Station; PGA/World Golf Hall of Fame in Pinehurst; Aberdeen Historic District; Victorian homes in Southern Pines; Midland Crafters; Sandhills Horticultural Gardens; and Cameron's Victorian homes and antique shops.*

Although the Sandhills are a wonderfully dense "country roads" experience—easy driving packed with interest—it's a deuce to organize a simple route here. First of all, this area is almost equidistant from Greensboro, Raleigh, and Charlotte. In other words, many people live less than two hours away and will follow completely different but equally interesting drives just to reach the starting line.

The next problem surfaces quickly: there is no logical starting place for a loop trip or a drive-through route. Touring yields to serendipitous discovery, backtracking, and return visits. You'll surely be tangled up following your curiosity.

The trick to enjoying a tour of this area is to somehow wiggle around long enough to not miss anything. This trip rides you round 'n' round. You can choose when to jump on or off.

Here's a bonus: the interstate highways don't go near the area, and the U.S. highways are tame expressions of commercial arteries. Venerable US 1 from Raleigh (variously two or four lanes, divided), which runs through Southern Pines, clearly qualifies as a rural route. So does US 15-501. Only after the two highways merge between Southern Pines and Aberdeen do they become urban-strength commercial. Regardless of how you come, you'll slow-lane into the Sandhills in a ride that has no drudgery.

We'll start from the western approach. Ellerbe, southwest of Southern Pines, is an uphill climb from Rockingham via US 220. The nine-mile drive is a rolling rural introduction to the southwest fringes of the Sandhills region.

Ellerbe presents itself demurely when approached from the south. Indeed, you will be downtown nearly before you have time to slow down. Ellerbe is virtually the geographic center of Richmond County, a small, mostly agricultural community where the hardware store still sells nearly everything you might need for the farm.

There are some twists in an otherwise straight passage through town that make stopping worthwhile, such as The Rankin Museum of American Heritage on West Church Street. This eclectic assemblage is the professionally displayed personal attic of Dr. Pressley R. Rankin, who, at eighty-plus years, still practices medicine in Ellerbe. The collection, which includes North American and African big-game animals, the natural and social history of Richmond County, and artifacts from Native Americans of the Great Plains and Southwest, obviously reflects the tastes of a general practitioner and not a specialist. A collection like this in such a small town is completely unexpected.

The Long-Needle Loop: Sight-seeing in the Sandhills

The central business district is along US 220. Horton's Furniture features handmade rockers. Timely Antiques fills one storefront at the corner of Page Street and US 220.

Farther north, on the east side of US 220, is a grounded caboose, which is even more noticeable because it is painted white. In summer, it is the home of McSuggs' Homemade Ice Cream. The name is a playful pointer at the Suggs' produce stand, which shares the same turnoff and sandy parking area along the highway. The peach ice cream comes personally recommended.

One mile north of downtown, past the state highway rest stop at the junction of State 73, is the real reason for Ellerbe. The Ellerbe Springs Inn and Restaurant is a spot of extraordinary charm and character. It was built in 1857 by Col. W. T. Ellerbe, originally of South Carolina, who inherited some 1,200 acres in North Carolina that happened to include a spring.

The colonel built the fourteen-room hotel to exploit the healing waters of the adjacent spring. The rambling, elegant old inn, visible from US 220, flourished until the Depression.

Several owners and remodelings have brought the Inn's history up to the present management of Ms. Beth Cadieu-Diaz, who operates it as a bed and breakfast (it also serves lunch). Consider rocking on the wide porch or visiting the springhouse, where local craftsmen display Sandhills wares. The dining room is open daily.

There's no mystery about the name of Fairview, since from this ridge-top community the land falls away to the west and east, and certainly in times past there must have been some remarkable vistas. A highway sign marks a side trip east on State 73 to the Sandhills Agricultural Research Station. This facility focuses efforts on the peculiar demands of growing conditions in the region, primarily benefiting the area's many timber and orchard operations. State 73, a lightly traveled road, is excellent for bicycles, and is also a prime shortcut to Pinehurst via the small community of Jackson Springs.

But we're continuing north on US 220 to the community of Norman, named for the lumber mill here. In winter the flat fields on either side of the road are typically planted in winter wheat, greening an otherwise austere landscape. To the southwest, outside of Norman, is a water tower, clearly the tallest thing around. The land here has the feel of the plains of Oklahoma; the horizons are void of tall structures and seem very far away.

On the north side of Norman is a small church with an unusual steeple; the architecture reminds me of an early-twentieth-century helmet. You enter into ghost orchards; tract after tract of peach trees were auctioned off in 1992. The weary-looking, untended trees give a forlorn look to the landscape, as does the old packing barn in disrepair.

Some of the land is on the mend, however, and you can see the clearings, indicating attempts to return it to productive use. Then, too, you can imagine men and dogs working the field edges, attempting to put up a covey of quail. The land has a ragged old field edge that says rabbit, quail, and fox live here.

Continue on US 220 north to the intersection of State 211 east, one of the primary routes into the Sandhills central area. Just after you turn on State 211, take your first left, one block, to a small farmers' market. Its bins are filled with seasonal local produce, especially fruit from nearby orchards.

It's eleven miles to West End, then you will parallel the tracks of the Aberdeen Carolina & Western Railway into Pinehurst. The history of the region is tied to the tracks.

State 211 introduces you to the gradations of the landscape like few other in the state: from flat sandy-loam farmland to rolling white sand hills where only turkey oak and

The Long-Needle Loop: Sight-seeing in the Sandhills

long-needle pine thrive naturally. Then, too, agriculture and recreation have stamped this region with their own unmistakable marks—pine plantations, turf farms, orchards, and golf courses.

In fall, the hybrid pine plantations along the road become threaded with the electric yellow of wild grape and the rosy glow of the characteristic understory, which can include wild blueberries.

The most remarkable landmark in the first few miles of State 211 is the magnificent barn of Sandhill Turf Farms—acres of putting green for purchase—lining both sides of the highway.

One mile past the barn, at a small produce stand at the corner of SR 1143, is a sign for Samarcand Manor. Turn south, cross the railroad tracks, and continue south for three miles.

At the railroad crossing you'll see your first healthy clumps of wiregrass, a native grass of the Sandhills. Fine bladed and thickly clumped, in a wild wiry way it is extraordinarily beautiful.

The ridge-top road passes an unnamed U-pick sweet potato farm with neat-as-a-pin fields. After the winter plowing the land looks rich; the soil lies flat, not clumpy and heavy looking like fields elsewhere in the state.

As the road runs along the ridge, multiple ridgelines recede from view, providing a glimpse of the topography of the Sandhills. An avenue of long-needle pines and magnolias signals the entrance to the grounds of the aforementioned Samarcand Manor, founded in 1918 as a vocational school for women, and now operated by the North Carolina Division of Youth Services as a correctional institute. It has all the visual hallmarks of a college campus—a legacy from its origins as a private school.

Return to State 211 and travel 300 yards north to the Inn at Eagle Springs, sitting behind a small, private forest of long-leaf pines and a bit of manicured lawn. It's a renovated 1922 private girls' school that has five rooms.

Continue east on State 211 to Eagle Springs, a railroad crossroads community. Turn right at the junction of State 705 (Eagle Springs Road) and double back to downtown Eagle Springs. Take the only road south about a quarter mile to the parking area next door to the abandoned Eagle Springs Presbyterian Church, which closed its doors in the late seventies.

The Eagle Springs Pottery is a small shop next door. A quarter mile behind the pottery along a narrow sandy and needle-covered lane is a small cemetery. There are headstones, pinecones, and the sound of the wind in the trees.

As for the name Eagle Springs, the postmistress of Eagle Springs relayed the local wisdom on that topic: "If you follow Eagle Branch Road to where the paved road ends and the dirt roads starts, there is a spring. Somebody told me a long time ago that an eagle flew over the spring and somebody shot it and that's how the town got the name."

It's five miles to Seven Lakes, where you'll begin to see the pastures that hint at the horse country of the Sandhills. Suddenly you pass the West End School and you arrive in the community of West End. The name refers to the town being at the west end of the Aberdeen & West End Railroad.

The main crossroads of West End is the junction with State 73, which cuts southwest to Jackson Springs, site of a mineral spring that developed as a resort in the nineteenth century.

Press on to Pinehurst, passing the junction of State 5, to the circle junction of US 15-501, State 2, and State 211. This is possibly North Carolina's most famous traffic circle; it may in fact be one of the only rotary traffic interchanges in the state. Stay hard right, exiting immediately right onto Midland Road

The Long-Needle Loop: Sight-seeing in the Sandhills

(State 2). Follow the signs to the PGA/World Golf Hall of Fame.

Even though golf came "late" (early in the twentieth century) in the evolution of the Sandhills as a resort, the area certainly became the spiritual center of the then-developing sport. Exhibits in the hall highlight memorable moments in golf history, with features on the professionals, amateurs, and citizens who have made the sport so popular today.

Here's a suggested entry into the village of Pinehurst. After Page Road merges into Midland from your right, look for Field Road; turn right and then immediately take your first left.

This should be Cherokee Road. It still seems to hold the intended ambiance of the village's early years, threading past elegant bungalows to wind you to the commercial and historical hub of this resort.

You might as well park the car on the sand parking area between the library and the village green. It takes a few hours to poke about Pinehurst. The winding network of roads is more appealing on foot or bicycle than by car, because the architectural details of the houses are more easily seen. Packed earth walkways sidle along the residential streets, becoming brick in the village. It's a tweedy but casual place worn well by the people who keep the village bustling between rounds of golf. Walking, window-shopping, and people-watching occupy an easy day. Rather than tell you where to look, I'll tell you what's behind the scenes.

Tuftstown has a proprietary ring to it, doesn't it? It's one of the dusty ideas thankfully brushed aside in the naming of this village.

Bostonian James Walker Tufts purchased 5,890 acres of sandy, eroding land, void of vegetation, in 1895 from Francis Allison Page of Aberdeen. Tufts was both visionary and imaginative. He created a brand-new place in the middle of his personal nowhere by building first a hotel, The Holly Inn, and then a town around it, which included a casino. The entire town was built in six months.

Tufts hired Frederick Law Olmsted, crafter of the Biltmore Estate and Central Park, to create "a village with open park spaces and winding streets."

So plan to wind yourself dizzy exploring alleys, streets, and stores. Scoot through the alley beside the handsome BB&T on Chinquapin Road and step into #10 Market Square—Grounds & Pounds. Linda Cox runs this unabashedly caloric coffee shop, serving "cappuccino, espresso, desserts, and conversation."

The landmark 1922 theater, once home of the performing arts, is a delightful minimall, with an apparel shop and a wonderfully eclectic home furnishings store. It also houses the Pinehurst Playhouse Restaurant & Yogurt Shop, a favorite local eatery with outside seating.

The village past breathes in its older buildings, such as the Holly Inn (1895), the first structure here. It's a vintage hostelry, gambrel roofed, with gables, dormers, peaks, and spires and no two rooms alike. The original casino building (1896) is now the home of Pinehurst Properties. The Pinehurst General Store (1895) houses shops and restaurants.

Three hostelries within the village offer rooms and dining. The Holly Inn (renovated in 1985) sets a formal table with a more casual price. Popularly priced settled-in comfort is the appeal of the well-known Pine Crest Inn on Dogwood Road, a year-round gathering spot for mellowing into the evening. For homeyness, try the more-than-century-old Magnolia Inn, a bed and breakfast.

Return to Cherokee Road (which exits the village by the theater) and follow it to Carolina Vista Road. If you look right, at the end of the vista you'll see the Pinehurst Resort, certainly worth a peek.

Cherokee Road leads to a traffic light after passing underneath a railroad trestle. Turn left at the light on Beulah Hill

Fairways among the long-needle pines

Road (State 5) to pass the old Pinehurst train terminal, on your left. Some very dressy private train cars will probably be sided at the station.

Slightly south the road forks. Stay right and you will come to the main entrance of the level oval of The Pinehurst Harness Track, another tradition for trotters and pacers. Since 1916, Pinehurst has been the winter haven for some of the top trotters and pacers in the nation.

Pinehurst was an equestrian center long before golf became popular, and the Pinehurst Hotel had a riding director. There were weekly equestrian events at the track, which were the main social events of the early winter seasons of the resort.

Renowned sharpshooter Annie Oakley instructed at the track, which is now on the National Register of Historic Places. In one sense, the horse remains before the cart here.

In fact, the Pinehurst Resort and Country Club and the Village Council are asking that the National Park Service declare Pinehurst, including several golf courses, a national historic landmark. They hope to receive approval in time for Pinehurst's centennial.

Stay on Beulah Hill Road, past several golf courses and through the small crossroads of Jackson Hamlet, paralleling the track of what today is the Aberdeen Carolina & Western Railway, to the village of Aberdeen and the junction of US 1 and US 15/501. Cross the highway and turn left on Poplar Street, then turn right on Main Street. This is downtown Aberdeen, the original settlement in the Sandhills troika of Aberdeen, Southern Pines, and Pinehurst, and always the working heart of the region.

The central portion of the town itself is an early-twentieth-century commercial center waiting for a movie script. The commercial strip is the center of the 100-acre, eighty-eight-structure Aberdeen Historic District, which features many

The Long-Needle Loop: Sight-seeing in the Sandhills

Victorian-era homes. The entire district is easily walkable in a couple of hours. At the railroad crossing, note the artful brick Union Station. Next door is the proverbial little red caboose, serving as a visitors center and the place to pick up a self-guided walking tour map of the town.

In the 1760s, Scottish Highlander John Blue settled this area, known as "The Barrens," because it provided such poor forage for livestock. Blue founded a town, Blue's Crossing; a church, Bethesda Presbyterian Church; and a Sandhills clan. One of his eleven children, Malcolm, would own more than 6,600 acres of land here.

Aberdeen boomed for the Page and Blue families. The Page family built the Aberdeen & West End Railroad, contributing to a period of unmatched wealth referred to in local history as the Blue-Page Era (1879–1929). Walter Hines Page, a scion of that family, became Woodrow Wilson's ambassador to England and a great benefactor of higher education. Legacies of the Page family abound. The Page Memorial United Methodist Church (1913) and the Page Memorial Library (1907) were both erected as memorials to Allison Francis Page and his wife, Catherine Raboteau Page.

Continue east on Main Street, then turn left on Blue Street past the exquisite Blue-Schloegel house. Built in 1888, the home is a splendid expression of southern vernacular architecture and is included in the historic district. The house was constructed by John Blue, who founded the third railroad in the community, the Aberdeen & Rockfish Railroad, which still operates successfully today, after more than 100 years. Past the homes, turn right on Bethesda Road.

You will shortly see the spectacular metal arched gates of the Bethesda Presbyterian Church, founded in 1760 by the Blue family. After passing through the gates, turn into the paired entrance roads of the cemetery and park.

At the cemetery entrance is an immense rock with the following slightly enigmatic inscription:

The earth goeth on the earth, glittering like gold.
The earth goeth to the earth sooner than it wold.
The earth buildeth on the earth castles and towers.
The earth sayeth to the earth all shall be ours.

This is the winnsboro-blue granite and gifted by the Rockingham Marble Works.

Interred in this cemetery are many of the early Highland Scots who came to America in the mid-1700s. There is more than one McDonald here, though many older graves are actually across the street from the small wood-frame sanctuary.

Ambassador Walter Hines Page and his wife rest here, and the graves of the Butler family are marked by tremendous stones.

The church building, which dates from the mid-nineteenth century, is hardly ornate, and crowds the edge of State 5.

Approximately one mile north of the church, on the corner of State 5 and Earnest L. Ives Drive, is the Malcolm Blue Farm, which dates from around 1825. This inconspicuous farmhouse and several outbuildings form a prim compound, which is the historic center of the Scottish settlement of the upper Cape Fear Valley. The Malcolm Blue Farm serves as an interpretive center for the life of the pioneering settlers of this area.

Continue north on State 5, bearing right, away from Saunders Boulevard indicators, until the road becomes North Fort Bragg Road (look for signs indicating County 2074).

Across from Highland Trails is the entrance to Weymouth Woods Sandhills Nature Preserve, one of the most magical spots in the state, perhaps the last remaining stand of virgin long-needle pine. This is a glimpse of the Sandhills before turpentining, timbering, and golf. It deserves and can absorb its very own day trip.

The Long-Needle Loop: Sight-seeing in the Sandhills

There are not enough good words for this preserve. The wind whispers with a music that is unmatched, a peculiarity of the long-needle pine forests, a sound that has given our language the evocative word *susurrus*. Nothing sounds quite like this natural lullaby. As for other sounds that naturally go with it, step inside the visitors center for their remarkable exhibit "Sounds of the Night."

Leave the Weymouth Woods on Fort Bragg Road, turning west on Connecticut Avenue Extension, which will carry you to Southern Pines, the last of the Sandhills troika. The road goes directly past Weymouth Center, the 1920s home of author James Boyd, who wrote *Drums*. Boyd and his wife, Katherine, were benefactors of the arts and the community; the house and grounds are a center of cultural events and open to the public. The house is operated by Friends of Weymouth as a regional cultural center, hosting a writer-in-residence program, lectures, and musical performances throughout the year.

In contrast to the planned zaniness of Pinehurst's roads and the wandering trading paths of Aberdeen, the grid of roads in Southern Pines is as rigid as an I beam, the legacy of a railroad engineer, wouldn't 'cha know.

The Seaboard Airline Railroad brought John Tyrant Patrick here in 1884. Amid the long-needle pines, which were continually felled for timber, he saw value in the clean air and dry climate as enduring assets.

Patrick purchased 6,000 acres and began to build a "Yankee village" on both sides of the track, with two streets, Broad Street N.W.-S.W. and Broad Street N.E.-S.E., paralleling the rail lines. Commercial buildings front on these throughways, and the cross street names ring like an early sales pitch—Delaware, New Jersey, Rhode Island—all of New England—plus Illinois, Indiana, and Wisconsin. Pennsylvania Avenue divides Broad Street into its northern and southern segments.

You can peek and boutique along the tree- and awning-shaded sidewalks exploring storefronts with artistry in the brick architecture. Plantings of live oaks, magnolias, azaleas, and pines border the train track, creating a linear garden through town.

Grab a cup of coffee or a sandwich at the Southerland Soda Shoppe & Coffee Mill, Ltd., at 154 Broad Street N.W., and admire the 1937 wall cabinets of this one-time pharmacy built in 1909. Visit Hawkins & Harness, at 132 Broad Street N.W., jewelers whose prize gem may be the 1925 bank building they have restored to its impressive original state, with marble and slate checkerboard floors.

You may wish to backtrack to the residential streets east of downtown—up the hill. It's a heyday of Victorian-era exuberance. The seamed tin roofs, architectural gingerbread, and distinctive carpentry echo resort origins in this charming town.

Leave Southern Pines on State 2 West, Midland Road, the scenic corridor between Southern Pines and Pinehurst. This is one of the most elegant stretches of road in the state. What paints North Carolina's Sandhills region in memory—far more than its famous fairways—are the magnificent long-needle pines. Their foot-long needles tuft upturned branches and then bow earthward in a lovely softness that slows traffic on this route.

"You can always tell a newcomer on Midland Road," observed longtime resident horse trainer Marcia Emerson of Pinehurst. "They drive ten miles an hour, just looking at the trees."

Sighing at the trees would be more apt; they are so wondrously different and so abundant that they stamp the Sandhills as a place apart.

Although only five miles separate Southern Pines and Pinehurst, the undulating roll to the road and the twenty-

The Long-Needle Loop: Sight-seeing in the Sandhills

five-foot median, once a trolley route from the train station at Southern Pines to Pinehurst, makes the distance seem far greater.

On either side of the road are the large homes of estates. The old Tate Farm, now a golf course, sports remnants of its original horse track fence as artifacts of an earlier era.

You will pass the low buildings of Midland Crafters, constructed in the 1920s as the dyeing and weaving operations of Anglo Tweeds. In December 1960, Midland Crafters opened, displaying traditional and contemporary American crafts. It is a show house offering top-quality work of area potters, weavers, woodworkers, leather crafters, and many other artisans.

Continue toward Pinehurst, turn right on Airport Road, and drive until you come to Sandhills Community College, home of the Sandhills Horticultural Gardens. The college boasts one of the best ornamental horticultural courses of study in the country, modeled on the British master gardener approach. The students and faculty have planted an impressive garden tour de force. The Ebersole Holly Collection is the largest in the East. The Sir Walter Raleigh Garden is a one-and-a-half-acre formal garden. The entire campus is a year-round joy if you are a plant lover. All areas are fully accessible to handicapped individuals.

Return to Midland Road. Double back toward Southern Pines and turn north on US 1 heading toward Raleigh. In about twelve miles look for the junction of State 24/27, and turn right toward Cameron, half a mile away.

Cameron is a crossroads community with a different slant to that term. The first road was literally a wooden toll road—the Fayetteville Plank Road, which crossed through here in the mid-1850s. The second road was a railroad—the Raleigh and Augusta Airline Railroad, which arrived here in 1875 on its way to Blue's Crossing (Aberdeen). The civil engineer who surveyed the railroad was named Cameron, and the town was incorporated and named after him in 1879.

Two important elements that made Cameron citizens wealthy are missing from the current surrounding countryside—long-leaf pine forests and dewberry farms. The pine forests were the source of turpentine and naval stores (tar for ships), which were transported by the plank road to Fayetteville, the Cape Fear River, and then to Wilmington. When the railroad arrived, the trees themselves were felled, and the dewberry-growing industry thrived in surrounding farms. During the early twentieth century, Cameron was known as the "dewberry capital of the world."

It was a bustling boomtown one road wide. Today, that road—Carthage Street—is a showcase of fine homes reflecting the eclectic tastes of the Victorian era and the bungalow style of the twenties.

In 1983, most of the main street properties from the railroad to US 1 were placed on the National Register of Historic Places. There's a new type of merchandising in the town as well—antique shopping. More than sixty dealers lease or own space and keep the collectible shopping trade pulsing with a snappy pace.

You might want to check the glassware at Miss Belle's, once the Murdock McKeithen house, built in 1892. There are eight rooms of antiques, an upstairs-downstairs of collectibles. Miss Belle's also offers a luncheon in the Tea Room.

In the middle of town (easy to find) is The Old Hardware, another shop brimming with antiques. Downstairs in the store is the Dewberry Deli and Soda Fountain.

Near the railroad tracks are two vintage stores, Cranes Creek Antiques, housed in the old Muse Brothers Store, and Crabtree & Co., the old drugstore. Next door is the McKeithen Store, once a "mercantile store," now another antique shop.

The Long-Needle Loop: Sight-seeing in the Sandhills

Return to US 1 and you're on your way home, via whichever way you may have come to the Sandhills.

In the Area

The Rankin Museum of American Heritage (Ellerbe): 910-652-6378

McSuggs' Homemade Ice Cream (Ellerbe): 910-652-5629

Ellerbe Springs Inn and Restaurant (Ellerbe): 910-652-5600

Inn at Eagle Springs (Eagle Springs): 910-673-2722

PGA/World Golf Hall of Fame (Pinehurst): 910-295-6651

Grounds & Pounds (Pinehurst): 910-295-8335

Pinehurst Playhouse Restaurant & Yogurt Shop (Pinehurst): 910-295-8873

The Holly Inn (Pinehurst): 910-295-2300

Pine Crest Inn (Pinehurst): 910-295-6121

Magnolia Inn (Pinehurst): 910-295-6900

Malcolm Blue Farm (Aberdeen): 910-944-3840

Weymouth Woods Sandhills Nature Preserve (Southern Pines): 910-692-2167

Midland Crafters (Midland): 910-295-6156

Sandhills Horticultural Gardens (Pinehurst): 910-692-6185

Miss Belle's (Cameron): 910-245-7042

Dewberry Deli and Soda Fountain (Cameron): 910-245-3697

7 ~ Lowlands Crossed by Highlanders

From Fayetteville head east on State 53/210, then take State 53 to Elizabethtown. Go south on State 87, then cross the Cape Fear River on State 11 north. Follow it to State 210 north, then State 53 north, then State 242 north and home.

Highlights: *Historic Fayetteville; unique landforms called Carolina bays, with their white sandy soil and long-needle pines; Singletary Lake and Jones Lake State Park; the Cape Fear River; Moores Creek National Battlefield; the two-car Elwell Ferry; and the recreational haven of White Lake.*

This tour begins in Fayetteville, a city that played a pivotal part in North Carolina's history. The route, which partly retraces the migration of the Scottish Highlanders who followed Neil McNeill up the Cape Fear River in 1740, is a pokey loop between the Cape Fear River to the south and the Northeast Fork of the Cape Fear to the north. Along the way lies the ecologically mysterious "Carolina bays" of Lake Singletary and White Lake, and other unusual habitats that have puzzled ecologists for nearly a century.

From downtown Fayetteville, take Clinton Road east across the Cape Fear River to the intersection of Cedar Creek

Tavern in Fayetteville

Road (combined State 53/210). Turn right on this five-lane road that passes through an area changing slowly from rural residential to commercial use. These not-too-lovely beginnings continue until you reach I-95.

If your rearview mirror allowed you to peer back two centuries to 1760, you would have been across the river from Campbellton, a busy riverfront settlement about thirty years old. Less than a mile inland was a very unusual location where two streams crossed and maintained their individual currents. People settled there, drawing water from nearby Cool Spring. These frontier outposts grew together to become Fayetteville.

Cross over I-95 and begin the country road journey on combined State 53/210 south and east. This is the type of countryside where loblolly pines are weeds and the fox grape races through the trees, electric yellow tracery in fall. In the roadside ditches where the tangles come close to the highway, the native cane, or bamboo, is visible, creating impenetrable tangles where it has thrived for years. This highway has widened lanes to accommodate bicycles: parts of the automobile route overlap with one of the state's designated bicycle highways, Route 5.

The brush suddenly vanishes and the horizon clears as you ride into "Monsanto," as local residents call this major manufacturing center on the route. The massive complex, and the industrial plant next door, is large enough to be a small community and dwarfs the road. It seems decidedly out of place.

Shortly after Monsanto, State 210 peels off to the left. Continue straight on State 53, following signs indicating that White Lake is thirty-five miles away; Elizabethtown, across the Cape Fear River, is thirty-three miles ahead.

The route seems unremarkable though delightful; there is little traffic, and you are making headway toward the coast. Suddenly, the road literally slices through what appears to be a low, tree-covered sand dune. The sand is so white that such a passage is unmistakable. The change in vegetation is equally sudden. Long-needle pine seedlings bristle out of the sugary white ground like so many green bottle brushes. Scruffy turkey oak—black-barked, knotty, and contorted—writhes beside it. In marked contrast to the tangled native woods or the orderly rows of pine plantations, these landscape interludes seem stressed and haggard.

To some extent they are. This group of plants is known as the xeric (for dry) sand rim association. The white sand you saw was actually part of the rim of a great elliptical bowl, more than likely only the southeastern rim of such a bowl, one quarter of its full circumference. The rim rings around a Carolina bay, an unusual landform dominant along this route.

Lowlands Crossed by Highlanders

These bays (there are thousands in the two Carolinas) are one of the most enigmatic environmental mysteries of the coastal plain, and you're in the middle of a region loaded with them.

Would you were a crow, or a hot air balloon—anything to be above it all—you would be better able to see the fascinating pocked landscape. Until the advance of aerial photography, Carolina bays were recognized as widely distributed, but the numbers and the predictability of the shape (always elliptical with the long axis aligned northwest-southeast) were hardly realized. Rampant speculation began immediately, and by the early part of the twentieth century there was a type of "Ripley's-Believe-It-or-Not" debate about the possible origin being the result of meteorite impacts. No meteorite remnants have ever been found, however, and the theory of origin now centers around an intricate pattern of wind erosion.

Peat moss is associated with most of the bays to a greater or lesser degree. Pollen grains in the peat deposits have provided a means for scientists to date the formations. The best information places their origin at some time around 40,000 years ago, coinciding with a period of glacial expansion named the Wisconsin Ice Age.

Still, late-nineteenth-century botanists and geologists knew something was up, for they had followed the lead of local residents and earlier botanists to locally name and identify many such "bays." To the person on horseback or on foot, these were places to be avoided; typically, the vegetation was so thick "that a rabbit would bounce off." The term *bay* came not from the concept of embayment, or semienclosed body of water, but from the predominance of certain plants with their characteristic bay-shaped leaf and, when such leaves are crushed, "bay" scent.

The white sand interruptions of the otherwise flat coastal plain landscape are remnants of the same system—the "dry" rims, or borders, of the bays. Not all bays have them, nor will all rims still have bays; many have been drained for prime farmland, but along State 53 and back again along State 210, you will pass through sufficient remnants to take notice. Then, too, you will pass houses constructed on elevated landforms adjacent to remarkably flat fields with no attending stream to account for the elevation change.

At typical car speeds, however, you are less likely to notice the intricate detail of the bays as much as you will notice the wisp of rim or an impenetrable wall of vegetation where a neatly plowed field suddenly ends.

This explanation is perhaps tedious, but it is the fact that you can see variety in the landscape along rural roads that makes the driving enjoyable.

Surprise! There is a choose and cut Christmas tree farm along the route. The native favorite from the flatlands was once the widespread red cedar and perhaps the rarer Eastern white cedar, which grows in boggy soil. But more careful growing can bring seedling white and Virginia pine to fuller, more suitable forms for Christmas tree use.

You come to Cedar Creek before you arrive at the community of the same name. The road dips sharply to cross the slow-flowing, tannin-stained water that seems darker than tea. Cedar Creek is literally a crossroads community that sprouted at the crossing.

In a few miles, you'll come around a turn and be driving directly toward a fire tower, the kind of object that catches your eye. The routes part ways here. Bike Route 5 goes straight on what is called the Old Fayetteville Road. Avoid the tower (just joking, it's not that threatening) and turn right to follow State 53. The road loops through a pine plantation, where the evenly aligned trunks of the adolescent supertrees flicker like rows of towering corn as you pass by.

The roadside provides hints of the characteristic mysterious geology of this corner of the coastal plain. Again, the road skews through the white sandy soil that typifies a sand rim, with its almost family groupings of long-needle pine: Papa, Mama, and baby pines amid the scruffy oaks.

The long-needle pine groupings put a grin on my face; the seedlings seem to hang around together as though they were reluctant to stray. In fact, the tree requires exacting conditions for germination. A must is bare earth. Following germination, the trees grow straight down for as many as five to seven years. They simply park for a time, and all that is visible is that wiry bottle-brush top. A group of them together looks like a group of up-ended scared cats, all but their tails buried in the ground.

The vegetation looks entirely different along waterways such as Harrison's Creek, where it tangles thickly to the edge of the bank, and the water itself is tea colored and very slack. Such waterways have an almost ominous air—places you would rather not be unless it's by direct order.

Should you make the drive in winter, you will notice a closely cropped browned look to pastures. This is a region where warm season grasses, such as Bahia and Bermuda, are more suitable to the arid conditions. They brown completely after the first solid cold spell, enhancing the sepia tones of the winter landscape.

In the pine plantations, the cover is, of course, pine needles, which to my eye is one of the most inviting of the natural covers. Here and there, the pine forest will be populated with live oaks—scrubby, tough-looking adolescent trees that hold their branches very low and become thickets.

One of the first lakes you will pass is the small, cypress-filled Jessups Pond, on the east side of the highway. At a glance, you will recognize this pond not to be a bay, but instead the impoundment of a creek that crosses beneath the roadway.

Shortly afterward the route enters Bladen County, sometimes called the "Mother County," because its boundaries in

Colonial times went to the Virginia line and because so many counties to the west were once part of it. It became a county in 1734.

The most surprising element along this length of highway is the Cape Fear Reservation of the Boy Scouts of America, on the west side of the road. The imposing entrance gates do indeed signal a "place" in a seemingly placeless passage.

But the route is not placeless, for you enter quietly into the community of White Oak. State 53 curves to the right. If you want to take the long way, continue straight. The spur abruptly ends at a stop sign on Gum Springs Road. On your right is the handsome Bethlehem Methodist Church. Turn right, go to the next stop sign, and turn left. This puts you back on State 53 in White Oak after a two-and-a-half-block detour.

Prominent in White Oak is . . . no tree in particular because the town takes its name from a Colonial citizen. However, there is a frame commercial building, named Old Country Store, and you will get no argument about the name from this traveler. The store is small and the selection of items is limited, but it's good for snacking, looking, and leg stretching. On the walls are mounted twelve heads of some of the largest white-tailed deer I've seen anywhere. You'll be forced to admit that for such a small community, White Oak has big bucks.

For an interesting detour, turn right in White Oak onto the old River Road. A historic marker at the intersection refers to Harmony Hall, the home of Col. James Richardson and one of the few surviving settlement-era homes along this segment of the Cape Fear River. It is now a private residence.

The first intersection you approach is Middle Road, literally the middle road between the Cape Fear River and the swamps of Harrison Creek, which you crossed closer to White

Oak. A left turn here will send you back to State 53, two miles south of White Oak. Continuing straight brings you to an intersection with Myers Street. Turning left takes you across the Cape Fear to the town of Tar Heel and the junction of State 87. This is one of those patriotic little detours that citizens ought to at least consider. The town comes by the name very honestly but late in the game, incorporating in 1887. This community was once the largest exporter of turpentine in the world, shipping it downriver to Wilmington.

Retrace your steps to State 53 and continue south. Those of you who have traveled the horse country of Florida and the countryside around Silver Springs will notice a similarity in the next few miles of the highway. The effect begins shortly after you drive through the community of Ruskin.

What calls those other latitudes to mind is the more pronounced roll to the topography (remnant bay rims, perhaps?), the suddenly broadening crowns of the live oak trees that have been allowed to grow in pastures, and, in winter months, the color and texture of the grazing land itself.

You will, alas, drive through Yorick on the way to the intersection of US 701, State 242, and State 41. From this intersection (and north and west of Yorick) are the lands of Jones Lake State Park, within the 35,000-acre boundaries of Bladen Lakes Educational State Forest.

The forest is a reclamation project, begun by the Civilian Conservation Corps, who built many of the roads through the exhausted cotton land. Economic hard times forced a relocation of residents with federal help. The worn and weary landscape required a makeover as well, and a rotation of long-needle, loblolly, and slash pine has been established.

You are never far from history in this region. Jones Lake was named for Isaac Jones, who gave the land for the county seat of Elizabethtown (his wife was named Elizabeth). Nearby

Salters Lake honors William Salter, whose wife, Bessie, before the battle of Elizabethtown provided the Whigs with the location of the Tory forces commanded by John Slingsby of nearby Lisbon. Singletary Lake is named for Richard Singletary, who received a land grant here in the early 1700s.

The 2,200-acre Jones Lake State Park includes the Salters Lake Natural Area. Both lakes typify a variant of the Carolina bay land form.

Jones Lake is gradually filling with peat and losing water capacity, a natural progression for a Carolina bay. The 220-acre lake is only about 34 percent of its original size. It averages nine feet deep; neighboring Salters Lake, 315 acres, has a similarly shallow and uniform depth. Because of the high tannin content of the water, both lakes look black.

Nearby White Lake and Singletary Lake are also water-filled Carolina bays, but instead of a peat bottom, they have crystalline sand bottoms, making the water very clear. More about these lakes later.

Follow combined US 701, State 242, and State 41 south across the Cape Fear River into Elizabethtown. One hallmark of the river through central Bladen County is the high bluffs, as much as seventy-five feet above the river. These bluffs, such as the one Elizabethtown occupies, became the site of houses and settlements. Notice the ravine that slashes up to the town from the river.

The town, which became established in 1772, is mentioned in the writings of William Bartram, who visited an uncle of the same name on his plantation downriver. More on Bartram later.

Elizabethtown is the seat of Bladen County. The compact downtown commercial hub still pulses; the parking spaces in front of the stores are full. Turn right at the stoplight, which is north on State 87/41, and drive through the next light. You'll come to Tory Hole Park on the right, which commemorates an event that put Elizabethtown on the historic map.

During the Revolutionary War, Elizabethtown was a Tory stronghold. On August 27, 1781, Whig forces engaged the Tories and pushed them back down the ravine and into the river, ending their hold on the town. The ravine has since been known as Tory Hole.

Reverse your route through town, then continue straight on State 87 south (Broad Street), parallel to the Cape Fear River. This area, part of the lower Cape Fear basin, was settled in the 1700s. A 1733 map of the region identifies plantation houses and clearly notes Hammonds Creek, six miles south of the community.

Just out of the commercial district, State 87 drops in elevation. On the left is a simple prominent wooden building, Trinity Methodist Church, which stands as a kind of bookend to the downtown.

The drive along State 87 is wonderfully easy, passing through agricultural and forest land, with small communities such as Bladen Springs (note the low land of the watercourses and the higher ground on which the small frame houses perch). Whenever I pass through small communities such as this, I get a sense that the modern road on which I'm driving overlays the historic route, if not the virtual trace of the original road.

Five miles south of Bladen Springs is Mount Horeb Presbyterian Church, founded before the Civil War. It is a handsome building, lonely against a backdrop of cutover woodland.

A father-son team of American botanical explorers performed significant work near here, a fact commemorated by a historic marker at the intersection of State 87 and a dirt road just a short way after Mount Horeb Presbyterian Church.

Naturalists John (father) and William (his third son) Bartram of Pennsylvania spent many years studying North Carolina flora and fauna using the home of William Bartram, the younger half-brother of John. The home overlooked the Cape Fear River from the west bank and was called Ashewood by the previous owner, John Baptista Ashe, around 1731. The location is noted on a 1733 map; references indicate that only a cellar excavation and some chimney brick remain.

John Bartram spent time here as the official botanist to George III of England. William accompanied him as an artist on several trips, eventually returning to Ashewood to help his uncle run a store. William, however, was more interested in painting the natural world, and the commercial enterprise did not fare well.

At the direction of Colonial governor Arthur Dobbs, who lived in Brunswick and first described Venus's-flytrap, Bartram collected and sent samples of the plants (found naturally only within a seventy-five-mile radius of Wilmington) via his father to the Royal Botanical Gardens at Kew. Eventually, William received a subsidy by which he was able to take his remarkable journey through the Southeast, collecting plants and drawing the plants and animals he encountered.

This tour has been all around the Cape Fear River but not actually on it. There are several access locations. The U.S. Army Corps of Engineers maintains three lock and dam facilities for flood control that have recreational access. The first, Lock Number 1, is north of State 87 in the community of East Arcadia; the state road leading to the lock, and the pool upriver from it, is a left turn off State 87. Fishing, boating, and picnicking are permitted. (Lock Number 2 is in Elizabethtown; the third lock is seventeen miles south of Fayetteville.)

South of East Arcadia, State 87 leaves Bladen County and enters Columbus County. Shortly you will see the intersection of State 11, which marks the beginning of the return trip.

Lowlands Crossed by Highlanders

But before turning north, continue slowly south on State 87 about half a city block, past a small wooded lot, to a gravel driveway on the left. Turn left and you will be facing an abandoned wooden church of great weathered dignity and unknown denomination. The surrounding graveyard is of greater interest.

As you face the church, walk to the west corner of the graveyard, which is filled with many old family plots. Here you will find a stone marking the grave of Elizabeth Hooper Watters, who died in 1811. She was the last surviving child of William Hooper, one of North Carolina's delegates to the first Continental Congress and one of the signers of the Declaration of Independence.

Return to State 11 and turn north. The highway crosses back into Bladen County and over the Cape Fear River on a steel truss bridge. Continue to the rural junction of State 210 and turn right.

What a change a few miles makes! Here the soil is extraordinarily rich looking where it's piled on ridges. There is a pronounced roll in the landscape, and the long-needle pine grows profusely. The farmsteads are simple and appear old. The route crosses over the Black River and enters Pender County.

The next bridge the road crosses is Moores Creek. About a mile farther, turn into Moores Creek National Battlefield.

Moores Creek is a small black water, backwater creek following a winding course through swampy terrain to drain into the Black River in northwest Pender County. The creek is important because of a bridge, once the only crossing for many miles. On February 27, 1776, at a relatively small military engagement here, Great Britain's effective authority in the colony of North Carolina was ended, and the journey to independence began.

The two hours it takes to see the entire eighty-seven-acre memorial is a lovely interlude in the drive.

You can still imagine bagpipes in the mist, which in winter cloaks the lowlands along the stream. The bagpipes belonged to an army of 1,600 loyalists, many of them Scottish Highlanders recruited by Royal Governor Josiah Martin, to restore order and authority in the openly rebellious colony. Martin offered 200 acres of land and twenty years' exemption from the inflammatory taxes that prompted so much dissension.

Under the leadership of Donald McDonald and Donald McLeod, the loyalists assembled at Cross Creek (Fayetteville) to march to Brunswick on the Cape Fear River north of Southport. They were to join forces with an army led by Lord Cornwallis and Sir Henry Clinton. Diverted by patriots, McDonald and the Highlanders marched south and east through the bays and swamps to reach the old Negro Head Point Road. This route to Wilmington, established in 1743, went to the only crossing of Moores Creek.

About 1,000 patriots, under the command of Alexander Lillington and Richard Caswell, beat them to the bridge and set up defensible earthworks on both sides of the creek. McDonald had to decide whether to fight or flee. Believing that the patriots were on his side of the bridge, he decided to attack.

During the night, the patriot forces retreated across the bridge, removing the planking and greasing the girders as they went. They aimed artillery at the bridge and tucked behind the earthworks. At dawn on February 27, 1776, with bagpipes shrilling, the Highlanders attacked in single file over the three greased girders into fortified positions. It was a rout for the patriots.

A replica bridge now spans the creek, although the remnants of the old roadbed and patriot earthworks are still visible. Two memorials command the field of battle. The first honors the only patriot killed in the fighting; the second honors the Highlanders, also North Carolinians, who "did their duty as they saw fit." An audiovisual display at the National Park Service visitors center tells the detailed story of the battle and displays weaponry from the period.

Return to State 210 and head west, continuing straight at the intersection with State 11. The landscape becomes one of familiar rolling sand hills, dominated by pine trees, both long-leaf and loblolly.

At the crossroads community of Colly, State 210 heads north (right). Stay on State 53 and Bicycle Route 5, which continue straight. These two routes circumvent an essentially roadless (except for logging/forestry roads) and historically impassable acreage that is packed with such evocative place names as Otter Slide Bay, Coon Kill Bay, and Big Bay.

State 53 is a lovely drive that comes to the community of Kelly, a small cluster of rural houses and civic organizations. There's a small post office, a women's club, and, just north of town, a cable ferry that crosses the Cape Fear River. Large trees line the riverbank, and the dark and slack water crawls between the bluffs of the banks. The Elwell ferry, a name honoring a pioneer family in the area, was the turn-of-the-century enterprise of Walter and John Russ, who built and operated it beginning in 1905.

The original ferry was people powered—polled across the river, against the current, then paddle navigated with the current to the opposite landing. This is according to ever-smiling Rudolph Spaulding, who with Ronnie Young currently operates the ferry. It is run by the State Department of Transportation and runs from sunrise to sunset. There are two small shelters on either bank. The crossing takes about fifteen minutes, and the capacity of the ferry is two cars. The crossing

Cross the Cape Fear River on the Elwell ferry

carries you to Carvers on State 87, slightly south of the Bartram historic marker mentioned earlier.

Return to State 53 and head north. You might recognize the agricultural and forested landscape as you enter the Bladen Lakes Educational State Forest, which you passed through earlier. Singletary Lake State Park appears shortly after entering the forest. State 53 passes very close to the rim of Singletary Lake, and you may get a glimpse of the lake through the trees. If you stop and drive into the park, you will find the bunkhouses and piers in the sand rim around the southeastern side of this clear bay.

More remarkable perhaps is the route of State 53 around the southwestern side of the lake. The road is the perfectly curving dividing line between the shrubby pocosin vegetation of the bays on the lake (east) side of the road, and the xeric, or dry sand, rim vegetation that is typical of these formations. The contrast is startling.

A few miles after Singletary Lake State Park, State 53 begins to circumnavigate White Lake, a similar water-filled bay that has long been a recreational haven. It's introduced by a sign welcoming you to the nation's safest beach. Unlike Singletary Lake, White Lake is glimpsed by looking past the recreational homes constructed in the sand rim around the lake.

White Lake was known for many years as Bartram's Lake because of a mill that William Bartram operated. The millrace was fed by underground springs. Bartram owned a considerable amount of land on the lake.

One of the noteworthy locations on the lake is a small camp where in 1928 the North Carolina chapter of Future Farmers of America began as the Young Tar Heel Farmers. The group organized to promote vocational agriculture in the school system and has maintained the camplike campus on the lake since.

The commercial portion of White Lake is signaled by billboards for White Lake Beach and Bath House. For many years, White Lake was the beach for those who couldn't travel to the coastal resorts. The White Lake Beach Club was literally the jumping-off point for those who wanted to swim.

The community of White Lake rims the eastern side of the lake. There are several campgrounds with tent sites and RV sites.

My grandfather used to journey here from South Boston, Virginia, for fishing trips, working the clear waters for bass and bream. My mother recalled the fact that the fish he returned with were not particularly tasty, having an "earthy" flavor. I cannot personally state that the fish do not taste good; but the story points to the longtime reliance on White Lake for recreation.

From White Lake follow US 701 north through blueberry country to the junction of State 210. In summer, the blueberry fields north of White Lake offer a pick-your-own dream. If you don't want to pick, then stop at one of the many roadside stands for a box of blueberries. Places such as Chancy Blueberry Farm outside of White Lake offer both opportunities beginning in June.

Slow down at the intersection of State 210 and US 701, also known as Hickory Grove Crossroads. On the northeast corner of the intersection is a small country store, Autry's Grill. It features a hunter's breakfast, grilled foods that are country delicious, and fresh homemade pies. Do stop and come away with some fresh coconut pie and a dose of sunshine from the fine ladies inside. Turn west on State 210, which compared to the other roads on this route is positively urban, possibly because this is some of the highest, driest ground in the area.

The junction with State 242 provides the opportunity to turn north. After you cross the Northeast River, which here is just a small creek, the countryside plays tricks on you, and the vegetation is much more reminiscent of the Sandhills. Continue on State 242 north to Roseboro, a charming little town that grew up with a railroad that is no longer. The road enters through a well-cared for residential section. It's small, folksy, and very lovely. The commercial center seems to be lively.

Head back home by bearing west on State 24 and following the road through Autryville, Stedman (named for a former president of the North Carolina Railroad), and back to Fayetteville, closing the loop.

In the Area

Bladen Lakes Educational State Forest (Elizabethtown): 910-588-4161

Jones Lake State Park (Elizabethtown): 910-588-4550

Moores Creek National Battlefield (Currie): 910-283-5591

Elwell Ferry (Elwell): 910-862-3396

Singletary Lake State Park (Kelly): 910-669-2928

8 ~ Down by the River and Back Up Again

From Wilmington head south on State 133, State 87, and State 211 to Southport. Take US 421 north to head for home.

Highlights: *Historic downtown Wilmington, with its stern-wheel paddleboat and the USS* North Carolina *Battleship Memorial; Brunswick Town State Historic Site; the Southport Maritime Museum and Fort Johnston; the car ferry to the Fort Fisher Recreation Area and North Carolina Aquarium; Zeke's Island National Estuarine Research Reserve; the Kure Beach Fishing Pier; Carolina Beach State Park; and a zoo.*

This countryside tour of the lower Cape Fear River valley starts on foot in downtown Wilmington. The city's waterfront quickly dispels the misplaced notion that North Carolina's major port is on the ocean. Nope, this is mostly a riverfront town, more in the tradition of Savannah than Charleston. For the record, the nearest breaking waves are sixteen miles away as the crow flies; if you follow the river, the nearest whitecaps are nearly twenty-five miles.

Start at the intersection of Water Street and Market Street (US 17, the historic coastal highway). This is the commer-

Down by the River and Back Up Again

cial and historical heart of the city and makes for wonderful walking.

If you want to see the river firsthand, climb aboard the *Henrietta II*, docked at the foot of Market Street in Riverfront Park. This is a stern-wheel paddleboat that plies the river for about an hour and a half, showing you the sea captain's side of the harbor and filling in some of the historical nuance that rides the tides along any coastal town.

After you see the city from the water, you have to see it on foot, so start a free-form exploration that takes in the attractions along the handsome promenade of the Riverwalk and Riverfront Park (note the star-spangled backdrop—the USS *North Carolina* Battleship Memorial). Whereas the waterfront presents a dressed-up new opportunity to stroll and enjoy the river, several blocks of Front Street, north and south of Market Street, provide the opportunity to see and explore an older architecturally rich city that still has a steady commercial beat.

From Water Street, walk north on Market to 3rd Street, then turn left and walk one block. This puts you at the historic seat of government in Wilmington and New Hanover County. On the north side of Princess Street is City Hall-Thalian Hall; on the south side is the old county courthouse.

City Hall-Thalian Hall is one building with two purposes—government and theater. The east wing of the building, with the much more subdued portico, is the home of the oldest theater company in America, the Thalian Association. Constructed between 1855 and 1858, the building is still used as intended; the theater's lavish interior hosts events throughout the year.

In contrast to the Classical Revival City Hall is the Romanesque county courthouse. Spend fifteen minutes inside to view an introductory video of Wilmington and the surrounding coast. Collect several of the self-directing fliers—

the most informative of which is entitled "Cape Fear Coast Guide Map"— and head down the hill to Front Street.

In its earliest years, the settlement that grew into Wilmington was part of the historic Port of Brunswick, named for the settlement on the south bank of the Cape Fear that is now a state historic site. Interestingly, Wilmington proper had its place in geography settled several years before it finally acquired its own name.

The story of the city's founding has the ring of a land grab about it. After Maurice Moore and other South Carolinians founded Brunswick in 1725, ignoring prohibitions from the Lords Proprietors about staking claims in the Cape Fear valley, opportunists from the Albemarle region of the state, led by Governor George Burrington, took some land across the river. They set up shop where you are now, sixteen miles north of Brunswick just below the confluence of the Cape Fear and Northeast Cape Fear Rivers.

When the town of Brunswick was torched by the British during the Revolution and never rebuilt, Wilmington, by default, became the state's major port and most important city. As nearly every port city on the southeastern seaboard, Wilmington has had its bouts of war, fire, and the economic cycles of success and stagnation—a history powerfully reflected in its physical appearance.

The railroad brought riches and power here, highlighted in the Wilmington Railroad Museum, at the northern boundary of the historic downtown. In fact, Wilmington was a terminus of the famous Wilmington to Weldon Railroad, considered the longest railroad in the world in the mid-1800s.

As you walk south along Front Street between Grace and Walnut Streets, you will pass the Cotton Exchange, a shopping complex crafted from old cotton warehouses. Built for the commerce of another era, where railroaders and shipping merchants shook hands and exchanged goods, the buildings are recycled for the commerce of today. You can wander

Down by the River and Back Up Again

through the multileveled enclosed mall to descend to the public parking lot along cobbled Water Street, or continue your amblings along Front Street, eyeing the architectural heritage of a vibrant downtown. Eventually, retrace your steps down Market to Water Street.

Wilmington surrounds you with a blend of old and new, most noticeable when you walk the downtown. This is particularly true as you walk south along the river to Chandler's Wharf at Water and Ann Streets, a shopping exchange and dining center housed in historic structures. It claims itself to be "five acres of nostalgic Wilmington," and the boardwalk that overlooks the river is both restful and wistful.

Decidedly uphill on Front Street is the elegant home of former Governor Edward Bishop Dudley, first president of the railroad and the first governor elected by popular vote in 1836. The house has a historic marker, but then the entire city seems to. There seem to be more historic markers here than in any other city in the state.

Hop in your car and drive north on 3rd Street, which is a connector to US 117/State 133, to the bridge crossing the Northeast Cape Fear River. After the crossing, turn left (south) following the signs indicating State 133 south. You will quickly cross the Cape Fear River, west of its confluence with the Northeast Cape Fear. Then turn left onto Battleship Drive to visit the USS *North Carolina* Battleship Memorial, berthed in the Cape Fear River. When you arrive, you'll see that you could have taken the water taxi over from Water Street in Wilmington, a delightful outing.

Nicknamed "The Showboat," the USS *North Carolina* was an Iowa-class battleship, sister ship to the USS *Missouri*. The *North Carolina* earned fifteen battle stars during World War II, participating in every major naval offensive in the Pacific campaign. When the ship was placed in mothballs and scheduled for scrap in the early 1960s, concerned citizens and officials raised the funds to provide her a permanent berth as a memorial. It is a magnificent restoration. There is a two-hour self-guided tour of the massive ship, which looms like a floating small town above the parking area.

Return to State 133 south and follow signs to combined US 17/US 74 west/US 76 west/State 133 south. The informational signs should direct you to Southport and the Brunswick Islands. Exit from the right lane onto State 133 south toward Southport. At the stop sign, turn left and you're on your way. The twenty-three-mile route takes you through the piney woods and low-lying lands of the west bank of the Cape Fear River—good riding, all of it. Before you reach a head of steam, pull the car over in Belville and read the cluster of historic markers—eight, I think—at the intersection. It's a flash-card reminder that this area was pivotal in North Carolina history.

The first several miles of this route pass residential communities serving Wilmington. Then the route seems to stretch and gain energy on the smooth, straight passage through the great expanses of space that belong to timber and paper companies. To the east, the river side, the ground is typically low, tangled, and marshy. Across the road to the west is the lush but drier upland forest typical of the coastal plain. At times the route runs through the white sandy soil that is home to the long-needle pine and turkey oak.

Except for scattered communities and clusters of homes, the route is distinctly wooded and uninhabited, so much so that the sudden appearance of the sign noting Orton is nearly unnoticed. Don't worry, if you overshoot the first exit, there is another left quickly. Exit here and continue on Orton Road, also called Plantation Road.

There are two features (three historic markers, I think) for one exit, Orton Plantation and Brunswick Town State Historic Site. Follow the signs to each. The road carries you east of

Down by the River and Back Up Again

Orton Pond, the dammed waters of Orton Creek, impounded in 1810. As you pass the lake, the earthwork dam, though overgrown, is visible through the woods.

Roger Moore, brother of Col. Maurice Moore, the South Carolina real estate venturer who founded Brunswick Town, built Orton Plantation in 1735. At that time, the house was far more modest, although the land holdings were vast. Orton passed to Moore's grandson Benjamin Smith, who became governor of North Carolina and who further developed part of the acreage as a rice plantation.

The house has been enlarged to its present, stately Greek Revival form in two stages. In 1840 a second story and an attic with portico were added; in 1910 two wings were added.

Orton is the only surviving plantation on the Cape Fear River. It echoes the grandeur of the Waccamaw Neck rice plantations of South Carolina. The old rice fields and ponds are still evident, and serve as a refuge for waterfowl. By far and away the major attraction at Orton is the twenty-acre formal gardens, which are open to the public throughout the year. Orton is the stereotypical "southern plantation," an image reinforced by the Greek Revival recasting of the manor house as much as the rice plantation that supported the residents.

A short distance from Orton are the ruins of a related town, operated as the Brunswick Town State Historic Site. On display are the excavated ruins of nearly sixty structures, a confederate fort, a parish church, and the graves of those who populated the state's earliest and most important deep water port, founded in 1725.

For nearly fifty years, until the British burned the community in 1776, Brunswick Town was the heart of the lower Cape Fear settlement.

A visitors center provides orientation to the site and showcases artifacts excavated from the ruins, but the highlight is to walk the site itself. Brunswick makes for a haunting stroll; only foundations are visible, with placards detailing the name, date, and possible configuration of the original building.

Brunswick Town is divided into two high areas overlooking the river; they are separated by Brunswick Pond, which was once a low, swampy ravine. The townspeople of Brunswick constructed a causeway for "front street," which led to the docks. This causeway impounded the waterway served by the springs that provided freshwater for the town. The immense earthworks next to the visitors center are the remains of the Confederate Fort Anderson, constructed to guard the Cape Fear River.

South of the pond are the exposed foundations along "main street" in Brunswick, including the known remains of a tavern. The ruins of St. Philip's Church, built in 1768, tower over other excavations.

There is a brief side trip to Russellborough from the parking lot at Brunswick Town. The ruins on display there are of a lavish home (by frontier standards) of royal Governors Dobbs (1750) and Tryon (1770). The latter vacated the location for a more ornate place named after him at New Bern. The British burned the home in 1776.

Return to State 133 south to continue to Southport. Within a short distance, the landscape changes dramatically to the high arid-looking Sandhill plant community, indicated by the predominance of pine trees and the fuzzy "cattails" of long-needle pine seedlings. The road follows a high dome of land, a broad ridge that is drained by Orton Creek to the south and Allen Creek to the north, dammed to create the 250-acre Boiling Springs Lake.

State 133 crosses a special U.S. government rail line. This track carries munitions and military hardware to Sunny Point Military Ocean Terminal, one of the most important arsenals for the U.S. armed services. Sunny Point occupies some

Down by the River and Back Up Again

strategic real estate on the Cape Fear River and is surrounded by an enormous wooded preserve.

State 133 and State 87 merge; after the two separate again, continue on State 87 to Southport. State 87 ends at State 211, a commercial road serving the beach communities of nearby Oak Island and Southport. Turn left on State 211 and drive the mile and a half that turns back the clock at least seventy-five years when you enter the Southport municipal limits.

State 211 makes a sharp left at the town's main intersection, routing over Moore Street (you won't miss it), but you should go straight, following what is Howe Street, to the water. You will have to turn, but notice that straight ahead, under an old cedar tree, is a humble wooden bench, the Whittling Bench, where the old salts of Southport once sat, whittled, passed the time, and passed judgment on matters of the day.

If there is a best time of day to be in Southport, it would have to be early evening in summer. The entire town strolls down to the Southport Waterfront Park to make sure that the Cape Fear River is still there.

Twilight along the Cape Fear—spent strolling or fishing—is one of the most alluring pleasures of this uncomplicated coastal community. Walking along the river and fishing off the pier are activities that could become a soothing addiction. So could Southport itself, the small river town that Robert Ruark made famous in his reminiscence *The Old Man and the Boy*.

Just before dusk, the towering beacon of the Oak Island Lighthouse blinks on. The most powerful light in the Western Hemisphere, visible twenty-four miles at sea, begins its nightly work signaling the danger of Frying Pan Shoals and the entrance to the Cape Fear River. On the other side of the river, at the horizon, is the squat tower of Old Baldy, the oldest lighthouse in the state and a fixture on Bald Head Island.

Bald Head Island is the name of a resort developed on the most southerly acreage of a once 12,000-acre complex of maritime forest, upland dunes, tidal creeks, and marsh that form the easternmost edge of the Cape Fear River. It is also the location of Cape Fear itself. A private ferry controls access to the resort, departing from Indigo Plantation, at the south end of Ninth Street in Southport. The resort sustains high marks for preserving the natural island topography and carefully planning the development, resulting in a very isolated, uncrowded getaway. The resort staff has also gone to great lengths with a sea turtle preservation and monitoring effort.

Southport

Down by the River and Back Up Again

Pelagic turtles use the beaches of Bald Head Island as a nesting site. The island staff was one of the earliest recipients of federal permission to tag turtles and officially monitor the nestings.

Southport itself is a wonderful scenic place to be lazy. It is small (population 2,500), and it drapes across your mind with the same easy sway as the Spanish moss that hangs from the shaggy live oak trees along West Street. You can crisscross the town's streets in half an hour; don't miss West Street, one of the loveliest streets on the coast.

Sleepy as it seems most of the year, Southport does explode for special occasions. It is the official headquarters of the North Carolina Fourth of July celebration, swelling the town to 40,000 people. It bears this distinction for two simple reasons: first, the town was supposedly the first in North Carolina to celebrate the Fourth of July and has been continually doing so longer than any other community; second, the North Carolina General Assembly made that official.

If you have time for just one stop, try the Southport Maritime Museum, at 116 North Howe Street. Mary Strickland, the director, and her husband, Wayne, are greatly responsible for putting the museum together. It details the history that the river swirled around Southport.

Another site you might want to check out is the Indian Trail Tree, which thrives in Southport's Keziah Park, at West Moore and South Lord Streets. As a sapling the tree was bent to create a loop, marking the trail along the river. Now a large tree, it still boasts its distinctive loop.

For a side trip to the beach, return to Howe Street (State 211), and head west out of town, the way you entered. At the intersection of State 133, turn south. This will take you to Oak Island and the beach communities of Caswell, Yaupon, and Long Beach in just fifteen minutes. It's all the island you could ever want.

Still, follow State 133 through the stoplight until you see the large beach access area on the right. If you can find a parking place, a swim is yours for free. Continue past this and you will enter the community of Caswell Beach, passing the Oak Island Light and the U.S. Coast Guard Station on your left (the old lightkeeper's quarters is on the right side of the road).

The road loops at a turnaround before a pillared entrance. This is the grounds of the Baptist Assembly, a private retreat owned by the Baptist Church, which previously had been the army's Fort Caswell (retired circa 1826). There are several intact gun emplacements from this historic fortification, reinforced during the Spanish-American War and again during the world wars. Between Labor Day and Memorial Day it is sometimes possible to secure permission to drive through and look at the fortifications and admire the conversions of the obvious barracks buildings into the offices and dormitories used by vacationing children attending the assembly on retreats.

Reverse your route to return to Southport, then follow State 211 when it turns onto Moore Street to leave town. One block north, spanning the land between Bay Street and Moore Street, is the 1748 one-square-block domain of Fort Johnston, constructed to guard the channel entrance of the Cape Fear. Somebody has been on guard duty here since the mid-eighteenth century. The brick officers' quarters (1804) is the oldest surviving building; it is now a private residence.

One last glance at the Southport past may be seen at the Old Smithville Burying Ground, on the left. It is marked by a wooden sign and a noticeable memorial obelisk to the river pilots who lost their lives at sea.

State 211 takes you to one of the best forty-five-minute rides in the state, the Southport to Fort Fisher car ferry across the Cape Fear River.

Down by the River and Back Up Again

The ferry angles northeast across the shipping channel of the Cape Fear; on some passages you might share the river with an oceangoing cargo ship. As you depart, look along the north shore of the creek where the ferry docks. You can see the old brick tower of Price's Creek Lighthouse on the north side of the protected basin. This tower was one of two that oceangoing vessels would align to navigate the Cape Fear River shipping channel. When the channel shifted, the light became obsolete, eventually superseded by precise channel markers.

As soon as the ferry clears its slip and pulls into the river, you will see the large docks serving the Pfizer Chemical plant.

You are free to move about on the small ferry. I suggest taking a box of saltine crackers to feed the gulls and terns hovering hungrily above the ferry's wake. On a calm day, the crossing is a pleasant respite.

The ferry skews the river quickly and soon approaches Federal Point, where it will dock. On your right will be two landmarks: a large mound of earth—an obviously elevated vantage point above the essentially flat coastal landscape—and, if the tide is low, a line of rocks curving south and back east. The first is the former site of a Civil War gun emplacement. The second is known appropriately as "The Rocks," a breakwater constructed by the U.S. Army in the late nineteenth century to prevent the shoaling of the Cape Fear River channel.

When the ferry docks, exit the loading area and turn right at the gravel lot where boats and trailers are parked.

This is the southern terminus of US 421. "The Rocks" project out into the Cape Fear River from this point for nearly four miles, eventually tethering into part of the marsh of Smith Island. To the east is the "Basin," a favorite shallow body of water for two diverse groups, clammers and windsurfers.

The Basin is part of Zeke's Island National Estuarine Research Reserve, more than 1,100 acres of islands, marsh, barrier beach, and tidal flats. The key to seeing Zeke's Island is either a boat or catching low tide, when you can "run the rocks" out to the island, which is a small sandy spit, supporting some shrubby growth of junipers, yaupon, and live oaks.

The "Rocks," however, are long and slippery—dangerous when wet. If you chose this adventure, mark your time wisely. The rocks are impassable at high tide, and you don't want to be stranded.

East of your location are nearly four miles of barrier beach, also part of the preserve. It is open to pedestrian and vehicular traffic.

Here's how you get to that beach. Drive north (technically, west) on US 421 to the sign for Fort Fisher Aquarium. Turn right. In just a few bends of the road you will see the sign for the Fort Fisher Recreation Area. There is an immense parking lot with an elevated concession stand and showers. The beach here is reached by a handicapped accessible ramp over the primary dunes. At the south side of the parking area is the four-wheel-drive access location. If you are properly licensed and have four-wheel drive, you may drive on the nearly four miles of beach extending south from this point.

After splashing around awhile, leave the parking lot and turn left to reach the North Carolina Aquarium at Fort Fisher.

Here's one of the best buys on the beach. You may watch skate swim (fly?) underwater or go nose to nose with residents of the 20,000-gallon shark tank. A new exhibit about oceangoing turtles with a model of an actual turtle "crawl," or track, details the life history of these endangered creatures.

There are nature trails as well; bug spray is advised.

Leave the aquarium and drive north until you reach US 421; turn north again and head toward Fort Fisher State

Historic Site. The road passes directly through the site. The entrance to the parking lot is across US 421 from an exquisite grove of salt-sculpted live oak and yaupon holly trees.

Fort Fisher was an earthwork fortification that fell to a merciless assault on January 15, 1865, the largest land-sea battle ever fought on American soil. The remnants of the fort are minimal; the ocean has already claimed two-thirds of the earthworks constructed by the Confederate soldiers to defend and maintain the port of Wilmington as a source of supply for the South.

An interpretive slide show and exhibits depict the fort's history. It is possible to walk through part of the parade ground and along portions of the earthen ramparts.

If you walk to the memorial flagpole at the oceanside turnout and look north along the edge of the surf, you can see a North Carolina Natural Heritage Site. Actually, all you can see is rocks emerging from the sand. It's the only natural rocky outcrop on the North Carolina coast, made up of coquina rock, bearing the fossil of the small namesake bivalve that lived at least 10,000 years ago. Such rock underlies this part of the coast, but this is the only location where it is exposed. It makes a very interesting beach, if a bit dicey for body surfing. . . .

Continue north on US 421, through the Fort Fisher gates and into the community of Kure Beach, an unpretentious beachfront town.

The community, incorporated since 1947, is a low-key, no-frills kind of place. Downtown Kure Beach, at the intersection of Avenue K and US 421, is one block west of the Kure Beach Fishing Pier. The pier was constructed in 1923 by L. C. Kure; he immediately rebuilt it the following year because it collapsed. In fact, the many rises and falls of the Kure Beach Pier make a yo-yoing story—up, down, up, down, and still up today—one of the oldest piers (with some of the newest parts?) in the state.

If you don't like crawling through beach traffic, turn west on Avenue K, then turn north (right) on Dow Road. This maneuver bypasses all of the congestion between Kure Beach and the Intracoastal Waterway bridge.

But if you drive through Kure Beach, you will pass the LaQue Test Center, a beachfront junkyard—that's the best way to describe it. This Department of Defense installation has metal racks for items that must be tested for their resistance to corrosion. Think of it as environmental art and you won't wince quite as much when you see it.

The next incorporated community is Carolina Beach (Hanby Beach and Wilmington Beach are unincorporated), a collegiately spirited place if there ever was one. You don't really sense the pulse of Carolina Beach when you approach from the south, since you have the option of turning right to reach the oceanfront. If you're arriving from the north during the season, well, good luck trying to make a left turn.

The center of the beach life is at the end of Harper Avenue, which loops around six parking places and six palmettos. East of those parking places, it's all coconut oil alleys and walkways, a very pleasant urban feeling that spills out onto a beachfront park—one of the most attractive oceanfront town centers in the state. In fact, Carolina Beach is really the only oceanfront community in the state that still has a "downtown feeling" beside the water.

The northern part of the community is a barrier spit, backed by Myrtle Grove Sound. At the extreme north end of town, you can take a four-wheel-drive vehicle out to Carolina Beach Inlet, which separates Carolina Beach from Masonboro Island. If you don't have a four-wheel-drive vehicle, try to find a parking space so you can walk to the inlet. This is one of the wildest spits of land adjacent an urban oceanfront (the north end of Carolina Beach is quite built up) in the state. It's a good hike to find shells in the off season.

Follow US 421 north out of Carolina Beach. Turn left at the intersection of Dow Road (there is a stoplight) and follow the signs to Carolina Beach State Park. It's one of the lesser appreciated but more terrific resources in the state.

The 1,773-acre park is at the confluence of the Atlantic Intracoastal Waterway and the Cape Fear River, a location that makes use of the recreational possibilities with a full-service marina for boaters. The most important purpose of the park is as a preserve for several unusual pockets of vegetation that might otherwise be lost in the crush of development.

The star plant in the park is Venus's-flytrap, which snares insects in wondrous jawlike leaves. It occurs naturally only within a seventy-five-mile radius of Wilmington. The plant, which thrives here, is one of the featured attractions of an interpretive trail. The peculiarities of the plant necessitate periodic controlled burnings in the park to create conditions favorable for the plant's growth.

This is also true of the long-leaf pine. The prescribed burnings make the park look rough for six months afterward, but it is a management strategy that is remarkably successful.

Although by now you may be at the end of a long day of adventures, you might want to park your car at the marina parking lot and follow the trail along the Cape Fear River, through the tangle of tidewater habitats, until you intersect with the spur track leading to the sixty-foot-high sand dune known as Sugarloaf Hill. The trail is one mile from the marina parking area to the dune, through the pure white sands with turkey oak and long-leaf pine. This is one of the few places in the state where you can easily visit such differing plant communities so close to each other.

The climax to the hike is the trudge up the Sugarloaf. This dune (there is an intrusive tree or two) commands the river and is a historic navigation landmark.

Leaving the park, you will cross over the Atlantic Intracoastal Waterway above Snow's Cut, which joins the Cape Fear River to the west with Myrtle Grove Sound to the east. Once on solid mainland north of the cut, you are heading toward Wilmington. If you turn to the left immediately after crossing the bridge, you can double back on the service road to River Road, which follows the east bank of the Cape Fear to Wilmington. Or you can continue north on US 421 to the Tote-Em-In Zoo, an eclectic private park that has more than 130 reptiles, mammals, and birds. This facility is widely noted for the curious nature of the collection, which bears the personal stamp of the founder, George Tegembo, who has such an eye for the unusual that he has filled several buildings.

Ask any local at this point how to return to Wilmington and they will tell you to turn left at Monkey Junction. This is the next major intersection north, where US 421 peels left to Wilmington and State 132 continues straight ahead to I-40 or US 17 north. Turn left on Carolina Beach Boulevard (US 421 west) and return to Wilmington.

One last but not least stop: Greenfield Gardens, on 3rd Street (which US 421 becomes shortly after merging with River Road). This park features a 180-acre lake that was once a millpond circled by a five-mile scenic loop. It is a simply lovely municipal park.

You will cruise back into Wilmington on 3rd Street, which is studded with historic markers, but then you read most of them at the beginning of the trip, didn't you?

In the Area

City Hall-Thalian Hall Center (Wilmington): 910-763-3398
Wilmington Railroad Museum (Wilmington): 910-763-2634
Greenfield Gardens (Wilmington): 910-341-7855
Henrietta II (Wilmington): 910-343-1611
USS North Carolina Battleship Memorial (Wilmington): 910-762-1829
Orton Plantation (Orton): 910-371-6851
Brunswick Town State Historic Site: 910-371-6613
Bald Head Island Management, Inc.: 800-443-6305 or 800-722-6450
Fort Fisher Recreation Area: 910-458-8206
North Carolina Aquarium (Fort Fisher): 910-458-8257
Carolina Beach State Park (Carolina Beach): 910-458-8206

9 ~ Water, Wind, and Sand: Along the Outer Banks

From Raleigh take US 70 east through Morehead City (147 miles), continuing 22 more miles to Atlantic. Take State 12 to the car ferry crossing to Ocracoke Island, then follow State 12 north along the island chain of the Cape Hatteras National Seashore through Dare County's beach towns north to Corolla.

Highlights: *Cedar Island National Wildlife Refuge; the ghost village on Portsmouth Island; Cape Hatteras National Seashore; the Native American Museum; lighthouses; windsurfing; Pea Island National Wildlife Refuge; the tallest sand dune on the East Coast; Kitty Hawk; and the Wright Brothers National Memorial.*

We will begin this tour with the eastern wind in your face, brackish water at your feet, and nearly all the rest of North Carolina at your back.

State 12 threads the narrow spits of sand that are the barrier islands of Carteret, Hyde, Dare, and Currituck Counties, with a smidgen of miles in mainland Carteret County. Yes, the islands in these counties are a portion of the Outer Banks (banks is a commonly used name for the collected individual islands that form this chain). The Outer Banks also properly include North and South Core Banks, Shackleford Banks, and Bogue Banks, but because the latter islands are

Water, Wind, and Sand: Along the Outer Banks

closer to the mainland—not as "outer" as the islands stitched together by State 12—they are generally not considered a part of the true Outer Banks.

This route traverses four counties, two ferry crossings, one bridge, two national wildlife refuges, and one national seashore, and passes by four lighthouses in its 125-mile passage. The Cape Hatteras National Seashore wraps 75 of those miles in its protective envelope; the remaining 50 or so miles belong to the oceanfront communities with such resonant names as Ocracoke, Frisco, Waves, Rodanthe, Nags Head, Kitty Hawk, Duck, and Corolla. Few North Carolina roads match the blend of wild surroundings, historical fascination, and austere beauty as the passage of State 12.

By map and odometer, this trip is a short run. Start fresh with a new day down east in Carteret County and you can certainly make Corolla in time to watch the Currituck Beach Light resume its nightly duties. My suggestion is for a more leisurely off-season run. There are plenty of accommodations when school's in session; the crowds abate, the fishing improves, and you can move a little closer to the folks who call these sparse islands home.

Plan to stop a night or two along the way. You can't quickly get your fill of these places by the edge of the sea. You better not delay the trip, though. Hurricane Emily sent a wet shock through the communities, soaking the furnishings of nearly every house from Hatteras Village to Rodanthe. The surging seas took a few homes in South Nags Head and chiseled the land from underneath State 12 at Buxton and Rodanthe. That's just the way it is out here.

The modest beginning for this trip is near the south boundary of the Cedar Island National Wildlife Refuge, 12,256 acres of undeveloped habitat. You'll cross a small slough that allows the waters of Thorofare Bay to flood westward with the tide.

There's a side trip right here at the start. US 70 continues five miles into Atlantic, a prim and lovely little community settled in the eighteenth century. Here is one of the prime jumping-off places—Morris Marina and Kampgrounds—for the isolated islands of Cape Lookout National Seashore. The Morris family, a National Park Service concessionaire, provides a car ferry to the islands, where they rent cabins. You'll need a four-wheel-drive vehicle on the islands, and because the cabins have just the bare necessities, you should bring everything you'll need. The location of the North Core Banks Cabins is about as wild as it remains on the North Carolina Coast—low, windswept barrier beaches with lots of sand, sun, and mosquitoes.

The shimmering bronze of the needle rush and cordgrass makes this one of the more spectacular expanses of marsh in the state. There's actually about 10,000 acres of marsh and slightly more than 2,500 acres of upland in this retreat, which is a strategic location for migratory waterfowl.

A good set of binoculars will make the marsh come alive. More than 500 species of birds have been identified here, and 270 species are regulars. The peak season for waterfowl is December and January.

Refuge headquarters are at the south end of Cedar Island on Lola Road. You can pick up maps of the refuge or arrange tours by advance request. The refuge is open during daylight hours all year.

If you ran out of road (State 12, to be exact), you're at the right place: Cedar Island, departure point for the steamer ferry to Ocracoke Island. There's not much around, but there is the Driftwood Motel and Campground. You'll also see signs for WhiteSand Trail Rides, where artist Wayland Cato has a stable of about eighteen horses for guided trail rides along the sound. You can ride the horses *in* the sound weather permitting.

Reservations for the toll ferry are recommended most of the year. You can reserve a space up to thirty days before departure; be sure to confirm it.

The two-and-a-quarter-hour passage is relaxing as you slip away from the mainland northeast to a place all its own in time and mood—Ocracoke.

Look south as the ferry crosses west of Ocracoke Inlet and you will see the low line of Portsmouth Island, the northeast end of North Core Banks and part of Cape Lookout National Seashore. Natives refer to it simply as Portsmouth, the name of the "ghost" village still standing on the island. There are twenty-five structures on the island, and until 1971 it was still occupied. When the last villagers moved off in that year, more than 250 years of continuous residency ended.

Portsmouth Village is in good shape and is on the National Register of Historic Places. One of the houses serves as a visitors center. The old church is the other building open to the public. Day trips and overnight visits from Ocracoke are possible. (No camping is permitted in the historic area.) The mosquitoes of the island are legendary. If you go, be wary! Park employees in the Ocracoke visitors center, at the Ocracoke ferry dock, will provide you with the names of people who can transport you to Portsmouth.

The Ocracoke Island ferry docks in the small harbor known variously as Silver Lake or "the Creek" by native islanders. This is perhaps the most enchanting and storied village on North Carolina's coast. It's a very small, very out-of-the-way location where life has always been conducted on "island time." About 700 people call the sixteen miles of Ocracoke their permanent home, living very close to one another since most of the island is Cape Hatteras National Seashore.

In fact, considering the remoteness of the island, settlement here is remarkable. As late as the early sixties, State 12

The ferry leaving Ocracoke

was not paved the entire length of the island, and many residents relied on cisterns to collect rainwater for drinking.

Although tourism is slowly altering the appearance of the island and certainly the rhythm of island life, Ocracoke is still insular. Just look at a map.

For more than four hundred years, Ocracoke Inlet has been the entry for ports on the central part of the mainland. The squatty tower of the Ocracoke lighthouse was authorized in 1823. Ocracoke village came about as an official site for the pilots who could navigate the inlet waters.

The early commercial success brought to these shores such free-spirited capitalists as Edward Teach. Better known as Blackbeard, Teach lost his head in a battle just off the southwest tip of the island.

Across the harbor from the entrance to Silver Lake are the peaked roofs of The Island Inn, one of the oldest hotels in the village and a traditional landmark. There are nearly 250 rooms on the island, a remarkable number when you consider the annual population. In season, that doesn't seem nearly enough, but in the off months, you can have most of the town to yourself.

When you disembark the ferry, you'll realize that you are in a "real" place instead of a three-month vacation village. State 12 swings around the north side of Silver Lake before winding east out of the village to the parking lots serving the beaches. By the time you see beach, you've left town; turn around and find a place to park. Ocracoke is for bicycles or long, leisurely walks.

As you stroll the shaded residential streets, you'll see physical evidence of the generational continuity that binds the island tight. Family cemeteries are scattered about the island, next to homes and businesses; past and future generations mingle freely. Gnarled cedar trees adorn front yards, and along some sandy lanes, live oaks throw a protective umbra across your path.

It might be fair to surmise that you can never visit Ocracoke just one time. It's a place to return to time and again. But if you are intent on passing through, there are a few must stops.

As you drive around Silver Lake, pull over at the Community Store, the island's longtime grocer. Ask directions to the British Cemetery, where four seamen from World War II are interred. This is one very placid reminder of the sea slaughter that raged offshore during World War II. The German submarine service sank so many ships that the area became known as "Torpedo Junction." The four seamen were crew members of the HMS *Bedfordshire*, sunk offshore in 1942. (You've already passed the turnoff for the cemetery, but the point is, talk to the natives; listen to that wonderfully lilting speech and vestigial accent.)

Wander over to the lighthouse, at seventy-five feet tall, a piker to the elegant lighthouses you're yet to see, but it is still in service. The light has recently been renovated, and the keeper's quarters house park service employees. By this time you've nearly looped through the village, and although you may have seen it all, you've barely scratched the surface of its personality.

As you proceed north on State 12, you will come to the "flats" and see the wind sock of the airstrip. The park service beach access location is visible directly ahead. Just beyond that is the Ocracoke Campground, the only campground in the National Seashore where you can reserve a campsite.

State 12 tracks about as far to the sound side as is possible on leaving the village. If you look seaward, you'll notice the low dune line. You once had to look out for wild horses crossing the highway. Not so now, but you may wish to stop at the pony pen.

Ocracoke Island's famous ponies fare better now than they ever did when they roamed free. These descendants of

Spanish stock probably arrived on the island after a shipwreck long ago, and at one time several hundred roamed free. Automobile traffic and environmental damage forced the park service to build a 160-acre enclosure, which gives them a source of water and the rich grasses on the sound side of the island. Now, though penned, the horses at least receive regular health care and are fed twice daily, an event that is open to the public.

The north end of the island brings another impasse, and for thirty-five to forty minutes State 12 is water bound at the ferry crossing of Hatteras Inlet. This is a lovely ride, accompanied by acrobatic gulls and terns that are adept at snagging crackers or food scraps flung to the winds off the ferry deck.

The ferry departs every half hour in season (less frequently during the winter months). First-come, first-served gets a seat, and if you miss the ferry, having to wait around the north end of Ocracoke isn't so bad. The flats to the east of the parking area are one of the best locations in the state to find the Scotch bonnet, the state seashell.

When you dock you'll be in the village of Hatteras in Dare County. You exit directly onto State 12, which would wind you through the town and hurry you on your way. Resist that temptation; turn right when you exit the ferry and use the public parking at ramp 55 (ramp is the National Park Service designation for public vehicle accessways). Nearly twelve miles due east from the dune overlook are the sunken remains of the CSS *Monitor*, which swamped while being towed from Hampton Roads, Virginia, following its spectacular Civil War "battle of the ironclads" engagement with the *Merrimack*.

State 12 wiggles through Hatteras in several languorous curves past the protected harbor, the several marinas, and several motels. You are nearly through downtown before you realize you're in the largest community on these fragile barrier islands. As you proceed through town, turn left at the Burrus

Red and White Grocery, an institution here since 1866. You will be on a residential street that is the solid heart of old Hatteras. Again, the wonderful pattern of life here places cemeteries next to houses next to small businesses.

State 12 crosses the "Slash," a small creek that marks the boundary of the village. From that point you are driving nearly due east to the village of Frisco.

Frisco is the location of the Native American Museum, an impressive collection of Native American artifacts and also home to one of the finest park service campgrounds you'll ever see. The road to the campgrounds is clearly marked, and the sites are perched amid a tremendous dune, with beach access to the sheltered waters of Cape Hatteras Bight. If you arrive here in time for dinner, stop at the Quarterdeck Restaurant.

After the campsite turnoff, State 12 leaves the ocean to ride through the forested portion of the island. Eventually, the small town of Frisco merges into Buxton, and you will understand why State 12 is the thread that holds the community together. Everything is along this roadway that sways through the surprisingly "hilly" island.

Buxton is the home of a world-famous landmark, Cape Hatteras Lighthouse, a 208-foot-tall barber pole–striped beacon. The entrance to the lighthouse visiting area is a quick side trip off State 12. Turn east; the road winds around a small pond to the lighthouse. It is at once both the world's tallest brick lighthouse and one of the most precarious. The sea beetles a scant 200 feet from its base.

There was great excitement here in 1993 because the National Park Service completed structural restoration to the 1871 tower, permitting visitors to ascend it for the first time in more than a decade.

Water, Wind, and Sand: Along the Outer Banks

Cape Hatteras Lighthouse

The old double keeper's quarters serves as a visitors center. One of the rangers is Rany Jennette, who grew up here. His father was one of the last light keepers.

State 12 winds past a softball field and several motels, seemingly gaining momentum for what it needs to do next—sprint the spit of Hatteras Island. At the city limits of Buxton the road turns back into the island's midpoint in one of the most storm-threatened lengths of the route. In 1993, Hurricane Emily took a swipe at the pavement, pummeling the dune line and gnawing at Buxton's direct link to the world.

Windsurfers brighten the waters of Pamlico Sound half a mile north of Buxton. Our neighbors to the north have made their mark on this particular "hole" of water, no more than three feet deep for nearly half a mile from shore. Named Canadian Hole, it's one of the hottest windsurfing spots on the East Coast. French is a useful second language here, particularly during fall when many French-Canadians arrive.

Now prepare to stretch like a greyhound as State 12 vanishes into the incredible one-point perspective to "shoot the skinny" of Hatteras Island. You will notice periodic breaks in the dune line—ramps for offshore vehicles that are spaced about every three miles, allowing access to accommodate surf fishermen.

I love the road north of Avon: you see mostly sky; the rest is flat land and water, all hypnotically picketed by the telephone poles that march endlessly forward. The landscape is so surreal that it seems part of a movie set.

Just when you think you are in the middle of nowhere, you stumble upon Little Kinnekeet Life Saving Station, established in the 1870s as one in a chain of havens every seven miles from Norfolk to Cape Lookout. The purpose of the service, the forerunner of the U.S. Coast Guard, was simple—walk the beach and rescue any shipwrecked mariners you see. So you aren't in the middle of nowhere after all—but the station crew was.

Three little villages—Salvo, Waves, and Rodanthe—slow your passage. You see a roof or two, a tree, then more trees tucked behind the dunes. Suddenly the speed limit drops and you're in Salvo. In midsummer 1993, someone torched the Salvo Post Office, the second smallest in the United States (eight by twelve). The villagers promptly rebuilt it, only to be denied the use of it by the U.S. Postal Service, because the reconstructed station had neither rest rooms nor a handicapped access ramp. Salvo residents pointed out, to no avail, that in their village of 150 people, nobody was handicapped, and that their own bathrooms were nearby. Eventually the

Water, Wind, and Sand: Along the Outer Banks

postal service agreed to a modification of their original hard-nosed ruling and gave at least a temporary stamp of approval.

In Rodanthe, on the oceanside of the highway, is the restored Chicamacomico Life Saving Station. During the summer, volunteers demonstrate old lifesaving techniques, similar to those used by the men of this station in their countless heroic rescues. The grounds of the station are open all year.

North of Rodanthe is the Pea Island National Wildlife Refuge. It offers winter shelter to a large population of snow geese that make these seven miles of beach a seasonal outpost. Parking places are clearly marked. The best viewing area is along the North Pond Trail, where a new access ramp and observation tower overlook a waterfowl impoundment.

State 12 traverses Oregon Inlet via the Herbert C. Bonner Bridge. As you soar toward the crown of the bridge, you can see on the oceanside of the highway an abandoned U.S. Coast Guard station. Heavy shoaling forced its relocation to a new multimission station on the far side of the inlet. The land will probably revert to the heirs of the original sellers, creating intense development interest in a very dicey place for permanent structures.

The bridge itself is over more land than water, due to shoaling and inlet migration since the year of the bridge's construction—1964. The north side of the inlet is Bodie Island. If you study a map you'll see that it is not really an island; well, it once was, and memories are long around here.

To the west of State 12 is the Bodie Island Lighthouse and Visitors Center, the official field center for the Cape Hatteras National Seashore. The 156-foot-high tower first blinked in 1872; it was the third light to serve Oregon Inlet, which was opened by a hurricane in 1846. In 1992, the park service

139

completed renovation of the light keeper's quarters as a visitors center.

State 12 becomes a serene passage through an evergreen shrub bog following the spur road to the lighthouse. In fall, wild grape glows electric gold in the foliage of wax myrtle trees, and grasses assume a flaxen hue.

Traffic comes to a tangled stop at Whalebone Junction, the vestigial place-name for what was once the intersection of the several old sand roads on the Outer Banks. Today it's a commercial hubbub, as US 64/264, US 158 bypass, US 158 business, and State 12 converge, cross, and go their separate ways. State 12, or Virginia Dare Trail, universally recognized here as Beach Road, goes behind the dunes. You should follow it by turning right; then slow down and enjoy the passage through Nags Head, Kill Devil Hills, and Kitty Hawk.

As you prowl State 12, you will move into an increasingly built-up environment, but you can still see the water, and you will develop a sense of how Nags Head evolved from its historic cottage origins to become a beachfront vacation town.

Keep an eye oceanside. Soon you will see about thirty very old wooden cottages. These are some of the original turn-of-the-century beach homes and are the historical heart of Nags Head. Distinguishing elements are the darkly stained wood, wraparound porches, and Bermuda shutters. The cottages have an unsurpassed dignity that has been adopted as an architectural form for newer structures as well.

Beach Road and the bypass nearly converge; to the west you will see an immense sand dune (408 acres) in Jockey's Ridge State Park. You have to climb the dune—it's the largest one on the East Coast at nearly 140 feet tall. Between the sand dune and Beach Road is Kitty Hawk Kites, home of the world's largest hang-gliding school. Owner John Harris has one dream—to make everyone free with flight. Lessons are conducted daily on Jockey's Ridge and are incredibly addictive.

While you're on the bypass, continue north a short way to the McDonald's Restaurant on the corner of West Ocean Acres Drive. Turn here (there should be a sign for Nags Head Woods), and follow the road even after the pavement ends. You will arrive at the parking area and visitors center for Nags Head Woods Ecological Preserve, a remnant eastern maritime forest owned and managed by The Nature Conservancy.

Return to State 12 through Kill Devil Hills, and continue north to the light at Ocean Bay Boulevard. Turn left here and cross the bypass to enter the Wright Brothers National Memorial. This is the spot where Orville and Wilbur Wright launched the age of flight.

Return to State 12 into Kitty Hawk; the road curves away from the beach at the Kitty Hawk Fishing Pier, then turns back toward the water into the private community of Southern Shores.

State 12 is anything but monotonous here; it runs behind the beach before diving into the dunes and crossing the island. You're sure to notice the fifties flat-top houses that mushroomed here—they're wonderfully juxtaposed to the newer oceanside estates.

I should tell you where you're going; you're going to Duck.

State 12 dodges some dunes, tunnels through maritime forest angling ever west, and slides across the island in a deliberate skew to Currituck Sound. Surprise! At an S curve, there's a sign for Duck—the beach that the Northeast craves.

Less than fifteen years ago, only 200 to 300 residents called Duck home, and there were only two places to buy sundries. What you see today when you visit is the best of the new-wave, designer-beach development. The appeal of Duck is that you can get away, but not so far away.

As you wind through the community, you'll leave the trees of such splendid shopping areas as Scarborough Faire and move into the dune flats. You'll pass the U.S. Army Research Pier. Finally, north of Duck, you'll come to the Sanderling Inn and Restaurant, the last stop in Dare County. This is the only inn out here, with sixty plush rooms and fine dining in the restored 1899 Caffey's Inlet Lifesaving Station, on the National Register of Historic Places. The dining is continental cuisine with high local flavor in the historic decor.

State 12 bends sharply past Sanderling and enters the Pine Island Sanctuary, a National Audubon Society preserve, which spans the western boundary of State 12 for nearly three miles.

Eventually you will begin to see more and more homes as State 12 winds north to Corolla, sandwiched between wax myrtles and red cedars.

When you see the Food Lion grocery and the water tower, you know you're closing in on Corolla. Finally, after the jarring visual amenity of a pitch and putt golf course, you'll see the Currituck Beach Lighthouse. Beneath it, hidden by the veil of trees, is the lighthouse keeper's quarters. This was the last of the giant Outer Banks lighthouses; it was completed in 1875 and is still operating. It is distinctive because it is unpainted. The grounds are open for walking, and between Easter and Thanksgiving you can climb the tower for a small fee. When you reach the top, you are metaphorically as far as you can go, in the light and on State 12.

Below you is the multigabled roof of Whalehead Club. Spreading south are the rich green woods that now grow houses. But look to the north, where State 12 can't go: there's fifteen miles to Virginia just like it always was, on the edge of the sea, between heaven and earth.

Water, Wind, and Sand: Along the Outer Banks

In the Area

Cedar Island National Wildlife Refuge (Lola): 919-225-2511

Morris Marina and Kampgrounds (Atlantic): 919-225-4261

Cape Lookout National Seashore (Morehead City): 919-728-2121

Driftwood Motel and Campground (Cedar Island): 919-225-4861

WhiteSand Trail Rides (Cedar Island): 919-729-0911

Cedar Island/Ocracoke Toll Ferry (Cedar Island): 919-225-3551

Ocracoke Visitors Center (Ocracoke): 919-928-4531

Ocracoke Campground (Ocracoke): 919-365-CAMP (MISTIX)

Ocracoke-Hatteras Ferry (Hatteras): 919-928-3841

Frisco Native American Museum (Frisco): 919-995-4440

Quarterdeck Restaurant (Frisco): 919-986-2425

Cape Hatteras Lighthouse and Visitors Center (Buxton): 919-995-4474

Pea Island National Wildlife Refuge (Rodanthe): 919-987-2394

Bodie Island Lighthouse and Visitors Center: 919-441-5711

Nags Head Woods Ecological Preserve (Nags Head): 919-441-2525

Jockey's Ridge State Park (Nags Head): 919-458-8206

Kitty Hawk Kites (Nags Head): 800-334-4777

Wright Brothers National Memorial (Kill Devil Hills): 919-441-7430

Sanderling Inn and Restaurant (Duck): 919-261-4111

Currituck Beach Lighthouse (Corolla): 919-453-4939

For additional information

Outer Banks Conservationists (Corolla): 919-453-4939

Hyde County Chamber of Commerce (Swan Quarter): 919-925-5201

Ocracoke Civic Club (Ocracoke): 919-928-6711 (map and directory listing accommodations and features)

Dare County Tourist Bureau (Manteo): 919-473-2138

Outer Banks Chamber of Commerce (Kill Devil Hills): 919-441-8144

Cape Hatteras National Seashore (Manteo): 919-473-2111

Index

BRIDGES, DAMS and LOCKS
　Herbert C. Bonner Bridge, Oregon Inlet, 139
　Cape Fear River Lock Number 1, East Arcadia, 102
　Footbridge, Spruce Pine, 10, 11
　Kimesville Lake dam, Kimesville, 67
　Orton Pond dam, Orton, 115

CAFES and GRILLS
　Autry's Grill, Hickory Grove Crossroads, 108
　The Bluffs Restaurant, Doughton Park, 41
　Cedar Crest Restaurant, Spruce Pine, 10
　Cosmic Coffee House, Blowing Rock, 22
　Dan'l Boone Inn, Boone, 24
　Dewberry Deli and Soda Fountain, Cameron, 90
　Ellerbe Springs Inn and Restaurant, Ellerbe, 77
　Fearrington House Inn and Restaurant, Fearrington, 72
　Four Eleven West, Chapel Hill, 70
　Gabriell's, Banner Elk, 31
　Grounds & Pounds, Pinehurst, 82
　Laurel Springs Cafe and General Store, Laurel Springs, 47
　Lee's Motel and Restaurant, Glendale Springs, 43
　Marion's Old Homeplace, Glade Valley, 48
　McSuggs' Homemade Ice Cream, Ellerbe, 77

145

CAFES and GRILLS (*cont.*)
Miss Belle's, Cameron, 90
Mountain Bakery and Restaurant, Glendale Springs, 43–44
Mountain Hearth Lodge and Restaurant, Doughton, 40
Pinehurst Playhouse Restaurant & Yogurt Shop, Pinehurst, 82
Quarterdeck Restaurant, Frisco, 136
Sanderling Inn and Restaurant, Duck, 142
Sonny's Grill, Blowing Rock, 22
Southerland Soda Shoppe & Coffee Mill, Southern Pines, 88
Sparta Restaurant, Sparta, 47
Spring Garden Bar and Grill, Carrboro, 70
CITIES. *See* TOWNS and CITIES

DAMS. *See* BRIDGES, DAMS and LOCKS

FARMS and MARKETS
Chancy Blueberry Farm, White Lake, 108
Hawks Produce, Sparta, 48
Morth Carolina State University agricultural experimental farm, Laurel Springs, 47
Pine Shadows Farm, Roaring Gap, 39–40
Sandhills Agricultural Research Station, Fairview, 77
Suggs' produce stand, Ellerbe, 77
Whiteside Pumpkin Center, Whitesides, 57

GALLERIES, MUSEUMS, SCHOOLS and STUDIOS
Appalachian Cultural Museum, Boone, 23–24
Appalachian University, Boone, 23
Blue Ridge Heritage Museum, Boone, 23
Cradle of Forestry, Pisgah National Forest, 63
Folk Art Center, Asheville, 2
Gardner-Webb University, Boiling Springs, 55

Index

Isothermal Community College, Mooresboro, 55
Clyde Jones' studio, Bynum, 72
Kitty Hawk Kites hang-gliding school, Nags Head, 140
Museum of North Carolina Minerals, Spruce Pine, 9
Native American Museum, Frisco, 136
Penland Gallery, Penland, 11
Penland School of Crafts, Penland, 11–13
PGA/World Golf Hall of Fame, Pinehurst, 81
Rankin Museum of American Heritage, Ellerbe, 76
Sandhills Community College, Pinehurst, 89
School House Gallery, Glendale Springs, 44
Silver Designs by Lou, Glendale Springs, 44
Southport Maritime Museum, Southport, 119
Wilmington Railroad Museum, Wilmington, 112

GARDENS and PRESERVES
Broyhill Park, Blowing Rock, 22
Annie Cannon Memorial Gardens, Blowing Rock, 22
Carolina Beach State Park, Carolina Beach, 125–126
Catawba rhododendrons, Roan Mountain Massif, 14–17
Craggy Gardens, Asheville, 3
Jenny Fitch's country gardens, Fearrington, 72
Greenfield Gardens, Wilmington, 126
B. Everett Jordan Lake, Farrington, 71
Nags Head Woods Ecological Preserve, Nags Head, 141
Niche Gardens, Carrboro, 69
Orton Plantation, Orton, 114–115
Sandhills Horticultural Gardens, Pinehurst, 89

GARDENS and
  PRESERVES (cont.)
  Weymouth Woods
    Sandhills Nature
    Preserve, Southern
    Pines, 86–87
  Zeke's Island National
    Estuarine Research
    Reserve, 122
GEOLOGICAL SITES
  Bat Cave, 61
  Blowing Rock, 21
  Carolina bays, 94–96,
    100, 106–107
  Chimney Rock, 58, 59
  Hickory Nut Gorge,
    Lake Lure, 58
  Kings Mountain Belt,
    Gastonia, 51, 52
  Looking Glass Falls,
    Davidson River, 63
  Mount Jefferson State
    Park, West Jefferson,
    44
  North Carolina Natural
    Heritage Site, Fort
    Fisher, 123
  Roaring Gap, 36–37
  Singletary Lake State
    Park, Kelly, 106–107
  Stone Mountain State
    Park, Traphill, 34–36
GRILLS. *See* CAFES and
  GRILLS

HISTORIC SITES
  Aberdeen Historic
    District, Aberdeen,
    84–85
  Alamance Presbyterian
    Church, Greensboro,
    66
  Bark-sided houses,
    Roaring Gap, 37
  Bethesda Presbyterian
    Church, Aberdeen,
    85–86
  Malcolm Blue Farm,
    Aberdeen, 86
  Bodie Island Lighthouse
    and Visitors Center,
    Cape Hatteras
    National Seashore,
    139–140
  British Cemetery,
    Ocracoke, 134
  Brunswick Town State
    Historic Site,
    Brunswick, 114,
    115–116
  Camp Alice, 7
  Cane Creek Meeting
    House, Greensboro,
    68
  Cape Hatteras
    Lighthouse, Buxton,
    136–137
  Carthage Street,
    Cameron, 90

Index

Central Shelby Historic District, Shelby, 53–54
Chicamacomico Life Saving Station, Rodanthe, 139
Church of the Holy Cross, Valle Crucis, 28–29
Cloudland Hotel site, Roan Mountain, 15
CSS Monitor, off Hatteras, 135
Currituck Beach Lighthouse, Corolla, 142
Depot, Spruce Pine, 10
Governor Edward Bishop Dudley home, Wilmington, 113
El Nido, Shelby, 54
English Inn, Spruce Pine, 11
Federal Point, Fort Fisher, 121
Fort Caswell, Caswell, 119–120
Fort Fisher State Historic Site, Fort Fisher, 122–123
Fort Johnston, Southport, 120
Guilford Courthouse battlesite, Snow Camp, 68
Gunter building, Spruce Pine, 10
Harmony Hall, White Oak, 98
Holy Trinity Episcopal Church, Glendale Springs, 43
Indian Trail Tree, Southport, 119
LaQue Test Center, Kure Beach, 124
Lighthouse, Ocracoke, 133, 134
Little Kinnekeet Life Saving Station, Avon, 138
Masonic Lodge, Pittsboro, 74
McBee Building, Bakersville, 13
Mill Point, Greensboro, 66
Moores Creek National Battlefield, Currie, 103–105
Mount Horeb Presbyterian Church, Bladen Springs, 101
Oak Island Lighthouse, off Southport, 117, 120
Old Baldy lighthouse, off Southport, 117
Old Smithville Burying Ground, Southport, 120

GARDENS and
PRESERVES *(cont.)*
Orton Plantation, Orton, 114–115
Port of Brunswick, Wilmington, 112
Portsmouth Village, Cape Lookout National Seashore, 131
Post office, Micaville, 8
Price's Creek Lighthouse, off Southport, 121
Roaring Gap Inn, Roaring Gap, 38
The Rocks, Fort Fisher, 121, 122
Rumple Presbyterian Church, Blowing Rock, 22
Russelborough, 116
Russel's Fort, Whitesides, 57
Carl Sandburg Home and National Historic Site, Flat Rock, 62
Spring Friends Meeting House, Snow Camp, 68
St. Bartholomew's Episcopal Church, Pittsboro, 74
St. John in the Wilderness, Flat Rock, 62

St. Mary's Church, West Jefferson, 43, 45
St. Mary's of the Hills Episcopal Church, Blowing Rock, 22
Sugarloaf, Carolina Beach, 125–126
Sunny Point Military Ocean Terminal, 116
Tory Hole, Elizabethtown, 100, 101
Trinity Methodist Church, Elizabethtown, 101
Turn-of-the-century beach homes, Nags Head, 140
Turn-of-the-century cottages, Rutherfordton, 56–57
USS North Carolina Battleship Memorial, Wilmington, 111, 113–114
Whittling Bench, Southport, 117
Wright Brothers National Memorial, Kill Devil Hills, 141

INFORMATION SITES
A Cool Glide at the End of the Ride, 64

Index

The Craggys, the Blacks, and the Highlands of Roan, 19
Down by the River and back up again, 127
The Long-Needle Loop, 91
Lowlands crossed by Highlanders, 109
New River Christmas Tree Country, 49
Old Greensboro—Chapel Hill Road and Some Extras, 74
The Ski Country without Snow, 31–32
Water, Wind, and Sand, 143–144
INNS and LODGES
Albert Inn and Lodge, 7
The Bluffs Lodge, Doughton Park, 41
Dogwood Inn, Chimney Rock, 59
Driftwood Motel and Campground, Cedar Island, 130
Ellerbe Springs Inn and Restaurant, Ellerbe, 77
Esmeralda Inn, Chimney Rock, 61
Fearrington House Inn and Restaurant, Fearrington, 72
Gingerbread Inn, Chimney Rock, 59
Hamrick Inn, Hamrick, 7–8
High Meadows Inn, Roaring Gap, 38
Holly Inn, Pinehurst, 81, 82
The Homestead Inn, Blowing Rock, 22
Inn at Eagle Springs, 79–80
Inn at the Taylor House, Valle Crucis, 28
The Inn at Webbley, Shelby, 54
Island Inn, Ocracoke, 133
Lee's Motel and Restaurant, Glendale Springs, 43
Magnolia Inn, Pinehurst, 82
Mast Farm Inn, Valle Crucis, 28
Mountain Hearth Lodge and Restaurant, Doughton, 40
North Core Banks Cabins, Atlantic, 130

INNS and LODGES (cont.)
  Pinebridge Inn and
    Executive Center,
    Spruce Pine, 10–11
  Pine Crest Inn,
    Pinehurst, 82
  Sanderling Inn and
    Restaurant, Duck, 142
  Woodfield Inn, Flat
    Rock, 62

LOCKS. *See* BRIDGES,
  DAMS and LOCKS
LODGES. *See* INNS and
  LODGES

MARKETS. *See* FARMS and
  MARKETS; SHOPS
MUSEUMS. *See*
  GALLERIES,
  MUSEUMS,
  SCHOOLS and
  STUDIOS

OUTDOOR RECREATION
  SITES
  Appalachian Ski
    Mountain, Blowing
    Rock, 22
  Appalachian Trail, Roan
    Mountain Massif, 15,
    17–18

Bald Head Island resort,
  Southport, 118–119
The Basin, Fort Fisher,
  121–122
Canadian Hole, Buxton,
  137–138
Carolina Beach State
  Park, Carolina Beach,
  125–126
Carolina Hemlocks
  Recreation Area, 7
Caswell Beach, Caswell,
  119–120
Chimney Rock Park,
  Chimney Rock, 59
Crosswinds Marina,
  Farrington, 71
Crowders Mountain
  State Park, Gastonia,
  51–52
Doughton Park, Blue
  Ridge Parkway, 41
Driftwood Motel and
  Campground, Cedar
  Island, 130
Fort Fisher Recreation
  Area, Fort Fisher, 122
Glen Burney Trail,
  Blowing Rock, 22
Jockey's Ridge State
  Park, Nags Head,
  140
Jones Lake State Park,
  Elizabethtown, 99,
  100

Index

Lake Lure, 58
Morris Marina and Kampgrounds, Atlantic, 130
Mount Mitchell Golf Course, 7
Mount Mitchell State Park, 3–5
New River Canoe & Campground, Sparta, 48
New River State Park, Wagoner, 46–47
North Carolina Bicycle Highway, Route 5, 94, 96, 105
North Carolina's Bicycle Highway, Route 2, 67
Ocracoke Campground, Ocracoke, 134
Park service campgrounds, Frisco, 136
Pinehurst Harness Track, Pinehurst, 84
Pinehurst Resort and Country Club, Pinehurst, 82, 84
Pisgah National Forest, 5–7, 63
Sliding Rock, Davidson River, 63–64
Stone Mountain State Park, Traphill, 34–36
White Lake State Park, White Lake, 107–108
Zaloo's Canoes, Index, 46

PRESERVES. *See* GARDENS and PRESERVES

RIDES and ROADS
Blue Ridge Parkway, 2–3, 5, 24, 34, 40–43
Elwell ferry, Kelly to Carvers, 105–106
Ferry, Atlantic to Cape Lookout National Seashore, 130
Ferry, Ocracoke to Hatteras, 135
Ferry, Ocracoke to Portsmouth, 131
Ferry, Southport to Fort Fisher, 120–121
Henrietta II stern-wheel paddleboat, Wilmington, 111
Steamer ferry, Cedar Island to Ocracoke Island, 130–131
Tweetsie Railroad & Theme Park, Boone, 23

153

RIDES and ROADS (*cont.*)
  WhiteSand Trail Rides, Cedar Island, 130

SCHOOLS. *See* GALLERIES, MUSEUMS, SCHOOLS and STUDIOS
SHOPS
  The Annex, Valle Crucis, 26
  Bubba's General Store, Chimney Rock, 61
  Burrus Red and White Grocery, Hatteras, 135–136
  The Candy Barrel, Valle Crucis, 26
  Carr Mill Mall, Carrboro, 70
  Chandler's Wharf, Wilmington, 113
  C & H Gas and Groceries, Greensboro, 67
  Community Store, Ocracoke, 134
  Cotton Exchange, Wilmington, 112–113
  Country Homestead Antiques, Sparta, 47
  Crabtree & Co.,
    Cameron, 90
  Cranes Creek Antiques, Cameron, 90
  Dovecote, Fearrington, 72
  Eagle Springs Pottery, Eagle Springs, 80
  Elly's Baked Goods, Banner Elk, 31
  Farmer's Hardware, Sparta, 47
  Greenhouse Crafts Shop, Glendale Springs, 43
  Hawkins & Harness, Southern Pines, 88
  Horton's Furniture, Ellerbe, 77
  Laurel Springs Cafe and General Store, Laurel Springs, 47
  Little Red School House, Valle Crucis, 26
  Mast General Store, Chapel Hill, 70
  Mast Store, Valle Crucis, 25–28
  McIntyre's bookshop, Fearrington, 72
  McKeithen Store, Cameron, 90
  Midland Crafters, Southern Pines, 89
  Miss Belle's, Cameron, 90

Index

Neese's Country Sausage, Greensboro, 65–66
Northwest Trading Post, Glendale Springs, 43
Old Country Store, White Oak, 98
The Old Hardware, Cameron, 90
Pinehurst General Store, Pinehurst, 82
Pringle Pottery, Fearrington, 72
Ray's Quick Stop, Eli Whitney, 69
Scarborough Faire, Duck, 142
Timely Antiques, Ellerbe, 77
A Touch in Time, Bat Cave, 61
Twisted Laurel Gallery, Spruce Pine, 10
SPECIAL EVENTS and THEATERS
Choose-and-Cut Weekend, Sparta, 48
Christmas Tree Weekend, West Jefferson, 45
City Hall-Thalian Hall, Wilmington, 111
Flat Rock Playhouse, Flat Rock, 62
Horn in the West, Boone, 23
North Carolina Fourth of July celebration, Southport, 119
Rhododendron Festival, Roan Mountain, 14
Studio Hop, West Jefferson, 45
The Sword of Peace, Snow Camp, 68
STUDIOS. *See* GALLERIES, MUSEUMS, SCHOOLS and STUDIOS

THEATERS. *See* SPECIAL EVENTS and THEATERS
TOWNS and CITIES
Aberdeen, 84–86
Atlantic, 130
Bakersville, 13
Banner Elk, 29–31
Bladen Springs, 101
Blowing Rock, 21–22
Boiling Springs, 55
Boone, 23–24
Busick, 5
Buxton, 136–138

TOWNS and CITIES (cont.)
Bynum, 72
Cameron, 89–90
Carolina Beach, 124–126
Carrboro, 70
Cedar Creek, 96
Chapel Hill, 70
Chimney Rock, 59–61
Corolla, 142
Doughton, 36
Duck, 141–142
Eagle Springs, 79–80
Eli Whitney, 69
Elizabethtown, 99–101
Ellerbe, 76–77
Estatoe, 8
Fairview, 77–78
Fayetteville, 93
Fearrington, 72
Flat Rock, 62
Frisco, 136
Glen Ayre, 14
Glendale Springs, 43–44
Hamrick, 7–8
Hatteras, 135–136
Hendersonville, 61–62
Index, 46
Jackson Springs, 80
Jefferson, 45
Kelly, 105
Kimesville, 67
Kure Beach, 123–124
Lake Lure, 58–59
Micaville, 8

Nags Head, 140–141
Norman, 78
Ocracoke, 131–134
Pinehurst, 80–84
Pittsboro, 74
Roaring Gap, 37–38
Rodanthe, 139
Roseboro, 108
Rutherfordton, 56–57
Salvo, 138–139
Shelby, 53–55
Snow Camp, 68
Southern Pines, 87–88
Southport, 117–120
Sparta, 47–48
Spindale, 55
Spruce Pine, 8–11
Tar Heel, 99
Valle Crucis, 25–29
West End, 80
West Jefferson, 45
Weymouth Center, 87
White Oak, 98
Wilmington, 110–113
Wilsonville, 71

WELL-KNOWN PEOPLE
John and William
    Bartram, 100, 101–102
Blackbeard, 133
John Blue, 85
James Boyd, 87
W.J. Cash, 55

Index

Thomas Dixon, 55
John Fraser, 4, 16, 39
Asa Gray, 45
William Hooper, 103
Reverend Levi Ives, 28–29
Thomas Jefferson, 45
Dr. Elisha Mitchell, 5, 24
Dr. Lucius B. Morse, 58–59
Annie Oakley, 84
Walter Hines Page, 85, 86
The Quakers, 68
Robert Ruark, 117
Carl Sandburg, 62
Thomas Wolfe, 24, 61–62
Orville and Wilbur Wright, 141
WILDLIFE SITES
Bald Head Island resort, Southport, 118–119
Cedar Island National Wildlife Refuge, Lola, 129–130
E-Z Ride Ass and Mule Farm, Greensboro, 67
B. Everett Jordan Lake, Farrington, 71
North Carolina Aquarium, Fort Fisher, 122
Pea Island National Wildlife Refuge, Rodanthe, 139
Pine Island Sanctuary, Duck, 142
Pony pen, Ocracoke, 134–135
Tote-Em-In Zoo, Carolina Beach, 126

Other titles in the Country Roads series:

Country Roads of Connecticut and Rhode Island
Country Roads of Florida
Country Roads of Hawaii
Country Roads of Illinois, second edition
Country Roads of Indiana
Country Roads of Kentucky
Country Roads of the Maritimes
Country Roads of Massachusetts
Country Roads of Michigan, second edition
Country Roads of New Jersey
Country Roads of New Hampshire
Country Roads of New York
Country Days in New York City
Country Roads of North Carolina
Country Roads of Ohio
Country Roads of Ontario
Country Roads of Oregon
Country Roads of Pennsylvania
Country Roads of Tennessee
Country Roads of Vermont
Country Roads of Virginia
Country Roads of Washington

All books are $9.95 at bookstores.
Or order directly from the publisher (add $3.00
shipping & handling for direct orders):
Country Roads Press
P.O. Box 286
Castine, Maine 04421
Toll-free phone number: **800-729-9179**